AF674723

STRATEGIC ESSAYS ON KASHMIR'S PIVOTAL YEARS

The 2002-2003 Inflection Point

ROMEET K KAUL

COPYRIGHT

Copyright © 2026 Romeet Kaul

This work is protected under the Copyright Act, 1957 (India) and international copyright treaties.

No part of this book may be reproduced, stored in a retrieval system, or transmitted in any form or by any means, electronic, mechanical, photocopying, recording, or otherwise, without the express written permission of the author.

Published by Saphor™ Partners, India

ISBN: 978-93-5655-450-4

Cover design by Diksha Kaul

First Published January 2026

DEDICATION

To my father, Shri Kundan Lal Kaul.

Despite the burden of his own struggles with mental health, he chose generosity, honesty, and kindness as the pillars of how he lived his life.

He was a man of quiet integrity—the kind of person who kept his word, treated others with dignity, and believed that a life well-lived was measured not by ease but by decency.

In a world that often mistakes toughness for strength, he showed me that true strength lies in compassion, in showing up for those who depend on you, and in facing your own demons.

This book, written from conviction and grounded in the belief that India must defend itself with clarity and resolve, is also a testament to the gentleness I learned from him. That combination—unwavering principle paired with human kindness—is what I aspire to carry forward, and what I hope these essays reflect.

Thank you, Papa. This is for you

Table of Contents

AUTHOR'S NOTE

This book brings together a set of essays written contemporaneously during 2002–2003, a period that marked a quiet but consequential shift in the political and security trajectory of Jammu and Kashmir. They were not conceived as a retrospective narrative, nor as an exercise in advocacy, but as attempts to understand events as they unfolded—often amid uncertainty, contradiction, and incomplete information.

The essays focus less on personalities or episodic crises and more on underlying patterns: the interaction between democratic processes and counter-terrorism, the recalibration of India's internal security doctrine, and the evolving relationship between violence, governance, and popular participation. Where judgments are offered, they reflect the context and constraints of the moment in which they were written.

Readers should note that this is not a comprehensive history of the Kashmir conflict, nor does it seek to resolve any long-standing political questions. Its purpose is narrower and, I hope, more durable: to document an inflection point that was visible in real time but only fully appreciated much later.

Minor edits have been made for clarity and consistency, but the substance and structure of the original texts have been preserved.

Romeet K Kaul

PREFACE

India's story in Jammu and Kashmir over the last three decades, as I have seen and written about it, falls into two very different epochs separated by a long, uneasy transition. The first was the bleak decade of armed insurgency and proxy war that followed the late 1980s, when Pakistan discovered that terrorism offered a low-cost, high-yield instrument to bleed India without inviting a conventional war. The second is the post-2014 era of constitutional integration and calibrated coercive response, marked by the abrogation of Article 370, the reorganisation of the erstwhile state as a Union Territory, cross-Line of Control surgical strikes, the Balakot air strikes, and, most recently, Operation Sindoor. Between these two stands the bridge-period of 2002–2003, when Kashmiris defied bullets to vote, a new coalition took office in Srinagar, and yet the architecture of Pakistan-backed jihad remained not only intact but emboldened.

This book is a product of that bridge period. I wrote these essays in real time in 2002–2003, when the guns had not fallen silent, voter queues snaked outside polling stations despite boycott calls, and Rawalpindi still believed it could have both nuclear weapons and deniable jihad as permanent tools of statecraft. Many of them first appeared in Kashmir Telegraph, the independent platform I founded and edited to document, analyse and contest the strategic narratives around Jammu and Kashmir. Others were carried, often in slightly different forms, by newspapers and portals such as The Indian Express, Asia Times, The News International, Mid-day, Daily Excelsior, Greater Kashmir, Kashmir Times, The Frontier Post and related publications that engaged with the region's politics and security. Together, they capture a moment when India's formal position on Kashmir was firm, its security situation precarious, its democratic experiment unexpectedly successful, and its strategic doctrine still trapped between rhetorical resolve and operational restraint.

The 2002 elections in Jammu and Kashmir were, in my judgement then and now, the first serious test of the Indian Union's democratic claim after more than a decade of insurgency, rigged contests and separatist boycotts. Despite explicit calls to stay away, threats from Pakistan-sponsored groups, and a long memory of manipulated polls, ordinary Kashmiris came out in large numbers, stood for hours, and chose ballots over bullets. Opinion surveys and field reports from that time showed overwhelming rejection of violence and clear majorities holding Pakistan responsible for the continuation of terrorism rather than New Delhi—a reality that sharply contradicted the propaganda that framed Kashmir as a simple morality play of "occupation" and "denial of self-determination". For me, the verdict was clear: the people of Jammu and Kashmir were asking for governance, not jihad; for development and dignity, not diktats from Muzaffarabad or Islamabad.

Yet I watched and wrote as the political and strategic establishment in New Delhi failed to fully translate this democratic mandate into a durable change on the ground. The Congress-PDP coalition that emerged from the polls was structurally conflicted: one spoke the language of "healing touch" and flirted with soft-separatist postures; the other belonged to a national party whose base demanded a hard line on terror and a clear assertion of national unity. The new state government experimented with conciliatory gestures—releasing detainees, signalling leniency, soft-pedalling security operations—but the militant infrastructure across the Line of Control remained intact, and foreign fighters continued to cross over. Pakistan's intelligence-military complex, having failed to delegitimise the elections through boycott and violence, responded by intensifying the jihad, targeting symbols of Indian statehood and Hindu faith from the Parliament in Delhi to the Akshardham temple in Gandhinagar.

It is this paradox that runs like a thread through the essays assembled here. On one side, 2002–2003 showed me that when given a reasonable chance at a fair contest, even a battered and traumatised population like that of Jammu and Kashmir will opt for constitutional politics. On the other hand, it demonstrated that democracy on its own, without strategic clarity and coercive credibility, cannot dissuade a hostile neighbour that sees terrorism as a rational instrument of foreign policy. In these pages, I move from the polling booths of Kupwara and Anantnag to the training camps across the Line of Control, from the coalition arithmetic in Srinagar to the calculations in Rawalpindi, tracing how a fragile local political opening was constantly sabotaged by a hardened architecture of cross-border jihad and by Delhi's own half-measures.

My central contention then, which I believe events since have borne out, was that what we were facing in Jammu and Kashmir was not a spontaneous revolt against injustice but a long-term, state-sponsored terror project engineered by Pakistan's military-mullah nexus. The rise of Islamist parties such as the MMA in the early 2000s, the cultivation of jihadi organisations like Lashkar-e-Taiba and Jaish-e-Mohammed, and the deliberate use of "azadi" rhetoric as camouflage for annexationist ambitions were, in my reading, structural features of Pakistan's strategic personality rather than temporary deviations. A state that outsources violence to proxies while sheltering under a nuclear umbrella leaves its democratic neighbour with an unforgiving choice: either live with perpetual terror or rewrite the rules of engagement. In 2002–2003, India had not yet found the political will to do the latter. It relied on diplomatic démarches, international pressure and moral argument, but still hesitated to cross thresholds or alter the script in any meaningful way.

The years since 2014 mark, in many respects, the belated policy answer to the questions that haunted those essays. What I argued in columns and analyses has progressively been codified into doctrine. The cross-Line of Control surgical strikes after the Uri attack in 2016 sent a clear message that India would no longer absorb cross-border terror without imposing visible military costs. The Balakot air strikes in 2019 drove that message deeper, showing that even training camps well inside Pakistani territory were not off-limits when Indian civilians and security personnel were attacked by Pakistan-based groups. Operation Sindoor, launched in 2025 as a direct and calibrated response to a series of major terrorist incidents, underlined that India's political and military leadership is now willing to adopt pre-emptive and punitive options at times and places of its choosing, rather than merely react on Pakistani terms.

Alongside this kinetic evolution came the constitutional shift that, in 2002–2003, many of us on the right of centre argued for but knew would invite fierce resistance. On 5 August 2019, the Government of India moved to abrogate Article 370, dismantle the separate constitutional dispensation for Jammu and Kashmir, and bifurcate the state into two Union Territories. What had long been described as a "bridge" between Kashmir and the Union was recognised, at last, as a legal and political firewall: it locked in a sense of exceptionalism, enabled a separatist ecosystem to thrive within an Indian constitutional frame, and constrained the Union's ability to enforce uniform norms of citizenship and sovereignty. The reorganisation of Jammu and Kashmir as a UT under direct central authority, combined with a sustained security campaign, has coincided with a marked decline in organised street violence, a significant reduction in local militant recruitment, and gradual improvements in key governance indicators, even if sporadic terror incidents and infiltration attempts continue.

From my right-of-centre vantage point, there is a clear continuity between what I wrote in 2002–2003 and what has unfolded since. Those essays argued that democratic participation alone, without integration and deterrence, would not neutralise the external drivers of jihad; that rhetorical toughness without action would be read in Rawalpindi as weakness; and that a divided constitutional status for one strategically vital border state was an invitation to permanent instability. The shift from "strategic restraint" to what may be called "strategic retaliation plus constitutional integration" has been, in my view, overdue and necessary. The revocation of Article 370 and the downgrading of Jammu and Kashmir to a Union Territory have gone a long way in arresting the rise of Islamist terrorism in the Valley and sending a message that there will be no semi-sovereign enclaves within the Indian Union. The surgical strikes, Balakot and Operation Sindoor, have signalled that cross-border terrorism will now invite calibrated but firm military responses rather than endless cycles of condemnation and calls for talks.

At the same time, I do not pretend that the story is complete. There is unfinished business in residual terror networks, in the persistence of "hybrid" militants, in efforts by Pakistan to probe for weaknesses, and in sporadic attacks designed to test India's will and unity. The full normalisation of Jammu and Kashmir—from a conflict theatre into a state of mind where integration is internal as much as institutional—will require not only vigilance and deterrence but also consistent investments in justice, development and political inclusion. Where I depart from some liberal readings is in my conviction that such normalisation must rest on an unapologetic assertion of national sovereignty and a clear constitutional hierarchy; it cannot be built on ambiguity about borders, equivocation about jihadist violence, or the myth that separatism is merely another shade of opinion within the democratic spectrum.

Why, then, bring out a collection of essays that were first written more than two decades ago, in a very different formal setting? My answer is that those years were the crucible in which today's consensus was forged. The inflection point of

2002–2003 exposed the limits of half-measures—dialogue without deterrence, elections without integration, security operations constrained by misplaced scruples, and a reluctance to match Pakistan's risk appetite. The analyses in this book anticipated many of the conclusions that now sit at the core of India's mainstream strategic thinking: that Pakistan's problem is structural, not episodic; that terrorism is a weapon of policy, not a cry of despair; that a special constitutional status for one border state distorts the entire federal balance; and that moral clarity must be backed by material capability and political will.

I write as a strategic and political analyst who chose to watch Kashmir from within, not as an abstract case study, and who founded Kashmir Telegraph precisely to challenge the false moral symmetry and lazy equivalences that dominated much of the commentary. These essays are unapologetically right-of-centre in their insistence on unity, in their scepticism toward separatist narratives and Pakistani claims, and in their belief that the Indian state has both the right and the obligation to defend its territorial integrity with clarity and, when necessary, calibrated force. They are equally candid, however, about Delhi's own failures in that period: policies that conveyed ambivalence, experiments in "soft separatism" that emboldened militants, and a political class too often content with managing the problem rather than solving it.

For the informed Indian reader—whether a citizen who has lived through the years of bomb blasts and bandhs, or a younger generation that has grown up hearing of Balakot and Article 370 rather than of rigged polls and the 2002 elections—this book serves three purposes. It is, first, a contemporaneous chronicle of a pivotal year, preserving how events looked before hindsight and official narratives smoothed them out. Second, it is an argument about cause and effect, tracing a line from the choices and hesitations of 2002–2003 to the strategic compulsions that produced the doctrines of the 2010s and 2020s. Third, it is a statement of conviction:

that the Indian republic, if it is to remain secure and coherent, must be willing to defend its constitutional identity and territorial integrity without apology.

The inflection point I wrote about in 2002-2003 did not, by itself, resolve the Kashmir dispute or end Pakistan's jihadist enterprise. But it revealed, more starkly than any previous moment, the gap between what the people of Jammu and Kashmir wanted and what Pakistan and its proxies were prepared to accept. The years since 2014—surgical strikes, Balakot, the revocation of Article 370, the UT reorganisation, and Operation Sindoor—represent India's eventual decision to close that gap on its own terms. This book is both a record of the argument for such a decision and a reminder that the work of securing and integrating Jammu and Kashmir, while now built on a firmer foundation, remains an unfinished task that will test the steadiness of India's right-of-centre consensus for years to come.

Romeet K Kaul
Pune
24th November, 2025

CHAPTER 1: JAMMU AND KASHMIR AT A CROSSROAD (2002-03)

When I look back at 2002-2003, I see it as the moment when Jammu and Kashmir stopped being only a security problem and briefly became a constitutional and political question again. In this introductory section, I set out the political and historical frame within which the rest of the book must be read. I argue that the 2002 assembly elections were not just another electoral exercise in a disturbed state, but the first serious test of India's democratic claim in Kashmir after a decade of insurgency, rigged polls, and separatist boycotts—and that the results exposed a fundamental gap between what Kashmir's people wanted and what Pakistan and its proxies were prepared to accept.

I begin by revisiting the long arc from the Dogra kingdom and the 1947 accession to the failure of UN-mandated plebiscite resolutions, Pakistan's refusal to demilitarise, and the gradual erosion of Article 370 from a temporary political compromise into a permanent alibi for exceptionalism. This history matters because it shows that by 2002, the constitutional debate had ossified while conditions on the ground had radically changed: an entire generation had grown up under the shadow of the gun, yet the legal fiction of "dispute" was still being used—mainly by Islamabad—to justify endless jihad. Against this background, the 2002 election emerges as a Himalayan turn: opinion surveys and turnout figures demonstrate that, when given a reasonably fair contest, Kashmiris chose ballots over bullets, governance over "gunpoint plebiscites", and local accountability over directives from across the Line of Control.

At the same time, I show that this democratic assertion

did not translate into strategic clarity in New Delhi or Srinagar. The coalition that took office—anchored by the PDP and Congress—was internally conflicted on first principles. One partner toyed with the language of "healing touch" and soft-separatism; the other was bound to a national party that could not afford to appear weak on terror or on the question of Kashmir's integration. In this section, I describe how well-intentioned gestures—releasing detainees, diluting the security posture, signalling "trust" to separatists—sent mixed messages to both Pakistan's generals and their jihadi clients. While the voter in Baramulla or Anantnag had effectively rejected Pakistan's veto over his political future, the state's own leadership hesitated to act as if that mandate had settled anything fundamental.

The Introduction, therefore, performs three tasks for the reader. First, it lays out the constitutional and historical scaffolding—from accession to Article 370—to show why 2002 was not just another election but a referendum on violence and separatism conducted within the Indian Union's own framework.

Second, it examines the actual verdict of that election through data and ground reports, underlining how sharply it cut against Pakistan's narrative and the separatist leadership's boycott politics. Third, it introduces the central tension that runs through the rest of the book: that a population can signal a desire for normal politics while external actors and hesitant policymakers keep the conflict trapped in ambiguity.

What follows in later chapters builds on this base. Once we understand that the 2002-2003 moment combined unprecedented democratic participation with an unbroken terrorist infrastructure and a divided coalition in Srinagar, the case for the later shift—towards Article 370's abrogation, full integration as a Union Territory, and a more assertive response to Pakistan-sponsored terror—becomes clearer. This Introduction is my attempt to fix that pivotal year in the reader's mind before we descend into the details of terrorist networks, Pakistan's internal contradictions, governance failures, and the eventual hardening of India's national security doctrine.

1.1 TREATY TO AK-47: COMPRESSED HISTORY OF JAMMU AND KASHMIR

A. Princely State to Accession (1846–1947)

In 1846, Gulab Singh purchased Kashmir from the East India Company for Rs 75,00,000 under the Treaty of Amritsar, establishing what we know today as Jammu and Kashmir. This purchase initiated the Dogra rule—a period marked by Muslim grievances against Hindu administrative dominance and eventual calls for democratic rights.

By 1931, Sheikh Abdullah founded the Muslim Conference to challenge Dogra misrule. The movement evolved. In 1939, Abdullah transformed it into the National Conference, deliberately incorporating Hindu leaders and secular principles. This reflected an attempt at composite politics—a vision that would later define Kashmiriyat.

When India and Pakistan gained independence in 1947, two pivotal moments determined Jammu and Kashmir's fate. On 22 October, Pakistan violated the Standstill Agreement, cutting off supplies. On 26–27 October, Maharaja Hari Singh signed the Instrument of Accession to India. Indian forces entered the state to repel Pakistani tribal raiders.

B. UN Resolutions and Article 370 (1947–1957)

India took Kashmir to the United Nations in January 1948, offering a plebiscite under UN supervision once Pakistani forces withdrew. Pakistan admitted to military presence in Kashmir, yet refused to withdraw. The UNCIP resolutions of 1949 laid out clear preconditions: Pakistan must withdraw first; only then could a plebiscite proceed. Pakistan never met these conditions.

Meanwhile, in October 1949, Article 370 was adopted—described as temporary, designed to give Kashmir special status pending a final settlement. What was meant to be provisional hardened into permanent exceptionalism, becoming the constitutional foundation for decades of legal and political ambiguity.

C. Elections, Accords, and Constitutional Erosion (1960s–1987)

The story from 1950 onward is one of repeated attempts to normalise Kashmir within the Indian Union, each blocked or undermined. The Delhi Agreement (1952) and the Kashmir Accord (1974) were Congress-backed accords granting autonomy, yet neither resolved the underlying tensions.

The turning point came in 1987. Elections were widely rigged in favour of the National Conference-Congress combine, galvanising opposition. The Muslim United Front, though unfairly denied victory, emerged from that election as a harbinger of Islamist politics. Within months, the valley erupted in armed insurgency.

D. Insurgency, Exodus, and Kargil (1989–1999)

In 1989, the Kashmir Valley witnessed the onset of an Islamist insurgency backed by Pakistan, marked by targeted assassinations and intimidation of the indigenous Kashmiri Pandit community. Facing systematic threats, killings, and calls for their elimination, Pandits were forced to flee the Valley in large numbers. The 1990 Gawkadal incident, in which security forces were forced to open fire on a violent mob amid escalating unrest, underscored the collapse of law and order in the region. By early 1990, the Valley had effectively been ethnically cleansed of its Pandit population, with an estimated 350,000 people displaced by Pakistan-sponsored terrorism and Islamist extremism.

The insurgency that followed was not homegrown. Within a decade, foreign militants in terrorist attacks rose dramatically. By 1998, 47 per cent of militants killed were foreign fighters—a statistic revealing Pakistan's central role in sustaining jihad.

The nuclear tests of 1998 altered the playing field. India and Pakistan now hold weapons of mass destruction, yet cross-border militancy continued unabated. When Kargil erupted in 1999—a 'contained war' that lasted weeks before international pressure restored the ceasefire—it signalled that even nuclear-armed adversaries could not deter Pakistani proxy tactics.

E. The 2002 Turning Point

By 2002, Jammu and Kashmir stood at an inflection point. After a decade of insurgency, militant dominance, democratic dysfunction, and Pandit displacement, ordinary Kashmiris were given a chance to vote. Despite boycott calls, threats of violence, and a decade of trauma, over 60 per cent turned out to vote. Opinion polls showed 90 per cent rejected violence and 72 per cent attributed terrorism to Pakistan. This electoral mandate represented something unprecedented in post-1990 Kashmir: democratic validation from within.

1.2 BREAKING PAKISTAN'S KASHMIR DELUSION

October 2002

Two credible opinion polls conducted recently on Kashmir not only corroborate each other, but their verdict on Pakistan is damning. MORI, a top British pollster, and the Asian Age-AC Nielsen opinion polls confirm the obvious - 60% of respondents want to vote in the ongoing election process; an overwhelming 90% state that violence is no solution; 72% say that Pakistan is behind terrorism in Kashmir; and, last but not least, 49% say that Kashmir is India's. These opinion polls have amply demonstrated that virtually nobody, even in Hurriyat Conference strongholds like Srinagar and Anantnag, wants the Kashmir Valley to go to Pakistan. This confirms that there is now a clear breach in Pakistan's grand delusion on Jammu and Kashmir

The overwhelming response to the electoral process in Jammu & Kashmir has clearly delivered a decisive blow to the secessionist elements and their masters in Islamabad. Despite large-scale killings of political workers and leaders across the state, voters have braved the bullets to turn out on polling day in large numbers to exercise their franchise. Despite strong words from the US, Pakistan could not stop itself from using all its dark resources to disrupt the democratic process, which in the end turned out to be a futile exercise.

Change is the essence of the democratic process, and the people of Kashmir are looking forward to change in governance - a process that is imperative to mitigate the suffering and hardships of the past decade under the most difficult circumstances. Analysts point out that it might not be a cakewalk for the ruling National Conference, which had hoped for a lower voter turnout, something that has favoured it in the past. It is now facing stiff competition from the Congress and the local entrant, the People's Democratic Party.

The low voter turnout in Srinagar bears ample testimony to the fact that the Hurriyat Conference still enjoys some confidence among the people; otherwise, its double standards and hypocrisy, exposed in other parts of the state, would have rendered it a complete non-entity. The people of Kashmir have categorically rejected the use of violence as a means of achieving their political objectives, which implies that they have accepted the democratic process as the instrument through which their genuine grievances will be addressed. Satisfying all these demands at once is, no doubt, a formidable task for any political dispensation.

Today, if the integrity of various institutions - the Hurriyat Conference and the company - has been battered, it is not the general public that is responsible; the burden lies squarely on the defunct political leadership. The successful culmination of the election process will usher in new hope in Kashmir. Pakistan should realise that the people of Kashmir have decisively rejected its gun culture and Islamist fundamentalism. They want to live in peace in a democratic set-up, with a way of life that is so close to their hearts - Kashmiriyat.

1.3 AFTER THE VOTE: CAN DELHI AND SRINAGAR WALK TOGETHER?

November 2002

With the advent of the PDP-Congress combine at the helm of affairs in the state of Jammu and Kashmir, federal democracy in India will be put to an ultimate test in a keen contest between the newly elected government in Srinagar and the BJP-led coalition at the Centre. The points of discord will be more than one, given the position of the combine, which many believe is opposed to New Delhi's official "Kashmir policy." Not only that, but there is also a deep divide between Congress and the PDP, and it is imperative that the duo evolve a common policy framework, given the ideological and political fissures between the two parties.

PDP is a derivative of the mainstream Indian political party, the Indian National Congress, and for many years Mufti Sayeed was perceived as the mainstay of the Congress in the Valley. However, given the political ideology he practised after disengaging from the Congress, the Mufti clan's party is seen in Indian political and diplomatic circles with scepticism for its pro-Hurriyat leanings; among many other issues, its description of the Kashmir problem as an "international dispute" is believed to be a major stumbling block that may hinder smooth relations with New Delhi. Contrary to New Delhi's position, it favours the immediate resumption of the dialogue process with Pakistan and the separatists, and the disbandment of the controversial Special Operations Group (SOG) set up to fight militancy in the state.

Centre-state relations have been of paramount importance for the ruling elite in Jammu and Kashmir when it comes to completing a full tenure. The National Conference, the historic political party of Kashmir, has never - political history testifies - governed the state when it has been at loggerheads with New Delhi. In the context of Centre-state relations, two historic agreements were put in place to evolve a mechanism for smooth functioning: the Delhi Agreement of 24 July 1952 and the Kashmir Accord of 13 November 1974, and in both cases, it was a Congress government at the Centre that signed these accords with representatives of Jammu and Kashmir. The Farooq Abdullah government, through its "autonomy resolution," tried to undo the Delhi Agreement, but the Union cabinet rejected the proposal.

The greatest triumph for Farooq Abdullah was his knack for completing a full term in power, but to make this possible, he went into overdrive to extend an olive branch to New Delhi, so much so that he did not even press hard on the autonomy resolution. In return, he was rewarded with unflinching support, even though Jammu and Kashmir was in a state of anarchy and, by any reasonable measure, was a fit case for the imposition of President's Rule by invoking Article 356 of the Indian Constitution. This in itself was Abdullah senior's greatest triumph, but it eventually facilitated his defeat in the elections.

The BJP as a party has had its share of setbacks in the elections, but with the Congress taking over the mantle of governance from the National Conference in Jammu and Kashmir, critics of the BJP-led NDA government at the Centre point out that the party has acquired a vital weapon to cross-check the main opposition party, the Congress, thus facilitating its full term in office in return for its support to the Congress-PDP government. However, should the need arise, if the coalition engages in practices that extend an olive branch to Pakistan or to the separatists in ways not in line with New Delhi's official policy, the situation, analysts warn, may assume turbulent dimensions. Congress, being from the mainstream of Indian politics, is also expected to act as a deterrent to counter the covert and overt manoeuvres of the PDP, should the need arise.

The history of coalition politics is not new for the Congress party in the state. Congress (I) in the past supported Sheikh Abdullah when he took over as chief minister on 25 February 1975. However, two years later, Congress (I) withdrew support to the Sheikh Abdullah government and, subsequently, except for a brief period when the Janata Party government was in place in Delhi, relations between New Delhi and Srinagar were at a low ebb. The Rajiv Gandhi–Farooq Abdullah accord of 1986 paved the way for the formation of a government on 25 March 1987. However, this accord, struck by the Congress to revive its sagging fortunes in the state, is seen by many as a key reason for its poor performance in subsequent elections.

Decentralisation and devolution of more powers to Jammu and Kashmir, political observers concede, are likely to gain momentum in the coming days, with the PDP–Congress combine evolving a common minimum programme before entering into negotiations with New Delhi. The combine must also undertake a complete revamp of the political and administrative machinery, which had collapsed, giving rise to joblessness, poverty, insensitivity, negligence and indifference. What has generated particular interest in politico-diplomatic circles, however, is the stand Congress will take on the issue of devolution of more powers to the state, and whether, in doing so, it will undo or undermine the Delhi Agreement of 1952 and the Kashmir Accord of 1974, both signed when Congress governments were in charge in New Delhi.

The fact that the coalition has to take into account the aspirations of Independents and smaller parties like the CPI(M), the Panthers' Party and others will, many believe, inevitably compound its problems, especially given that they come from diverse backgrounds. Much depends, analysts observe, on the composition of this "third front" within the coalition government. The will and commitment of the combine will also be tested to the hilt when it comes to negotiating with New Delhi on its demand for devolution of more powers to Jammu and Kashmir, something the BJP will not concede easily.

Kashmir, detractors of New Delhi argue, has not been handled properly, and Delhi has gone wrong again and again in the past. New Delhi must adopt a more conciliatory approach towards the new regime in Jammu and Kashmir and provide it with all necessary support to bring the violence-ravaged Valley back to normal - even if that requires making a few concessions here and there.

1.4 HURRIYAT'S MISSED MOMENT: PARTICIPATE OR PERISH

May 2002

In September–October 2002, Jammu and Kashmir, the only Muslim-majority state of the Indian Union, is scheduled to go to the polls, an event keenly awaited in political and diplomatic circles. Recent reports of hectic behind-the-scenes parleys to persuade the Hurriyat Conference to participate in the elections have generated considerable interest. New Delhi has opened channels of communication with the Hurriyat Conference, with senior official Wajahat Habibullah tasked specifically with convincing Hurriyat leaders to take part in the forthcoming elections. He has held wide-ranging discussions with Hurriyat chairman Abdul Gani Bhat and other leaders, but the initial reaction has been unenthusiastic.

For quite some time, serious doubts have been raised about the representative character of the Hurriyat Conference, which, according to many, is essentially a representative organisation of Sunni Muslims, lacking participation from other state minorities such as Hindus, Sikhs, Christians, Buddhists and others. The 1987 state Assembly elections, widely regarded as rigged, saw the Muslim United Front (MUF) - locally known as Muslim Muthahida Mahaz - as a coalition of opposition parties robbed of any realistic chance of winning seats. Although it is unlikely that the MUF would have won more than a dozen constituencies, it would have become a political force capable of pushing state politics in a more pluralist direction. The year 1996 saw elections to the Indian Parliament in May and to the state Assembly in September. While both the National Conference and the Hurriyat Conference boycotted the former, the latter saw the participation of the National Conference, which campaigned on a "maximum autonomy" platform. By again boycotting the polls and calling for a boycott in the Valley, the Hurriyat Conference was primarily responsible for the low voter turn-out; the National Conference government was elected with Farooq Abdullah as chief minister.

Hurriyat leaders are tempted to participate in the forthcoming elections, provided these are part of a wider process leading to a negotiated settlement of the Kashmir issue. Mirwaiz Moulvi Omar Farooq, a prominent leader and former Hurriyat Conference chairman, has said the elections would only help if they form part of a process aimed at a final settlement. Other Hurriyat Conference leaders - Prof Abdul Ghani Bhat, Abdul Gani Lone and Abbas Ansari - echo similar views. However, they insist that any negotiated settlement should be in accordance with United Nations resolutions, which, in their view, best preserve the dignity and honour of the people of Kashmir. Analysts point out that this insistence on a UN-resolution framework is the main stumbling block in achieving a breakthrough in talks with the Hurriyat Conference.

The strongest critics of the Hurriyat Conference argue that discussions with the conglomerate on election participation are futile because such a step sidelines Pakistan's role in the Kashmir issue. One analyst notes that, since the Hurriyat Conference functions on the explicit instructions of the Pakistani establishment, expecting it to contribute meaningfully to normalising the Valley and lending credibility to the Assembly polls by joining the fray is unrealistic. The latest Hurriyat Conference move to constitute its own "election commission" for conducting elections throughout Jammu and Kashmir, including Pakistan-occupied Kashmir (Pakistan-occupied Kashmir), to establish its representative character for any future tripartite talks, is seen by many as an attempt to achieve two goals: first, to neutralise the National Kashmir Committee under former Pakistan-occupied Kashmir president Sardar Abdul Qayoom, and second, to stay in contention and maintain pressure on New Delhi to kick-start a political process.

Many in politico-diplomatic circles also see this as a crucial year for the 65-year-old chief minister of Jammu and Kashmir. The National Conference's inability to make headway with its autonomy package and its decision to join the BJP-led government at the Centre, along with rampant corruption, have not gone down well with Kashmiris. Nevertheless, Abdullah, who reportedly harbours ambitions of becoming president (or even vice-president), is putting up a bold front and uses every opportunity to dare the Hurriyat Conference to contest the forthcoming elections. India must ensure free and fair Assembly elections and, to carry conviction with Kashmiris and the world at large, should not hesitate to invite independent international observers to oversee the process. Many countries have done this, and it does not compromise sovereignty. A broad process of reconciliation with ordinary Kashmiris must be undertaken to end the strife in the Valley, a process that many believe can restore peace and prosperity to the conflict-torn region.

The Hurriyat Conference now has a golden opportunity to seize the initiative. Abjuring violence is a long-overdue step the Hurriyat should have taken years ago, but it would still be welcome if it places these militant-linked political leaders on the side fighting terrorism rather than abetting it. The political process in the state must now seek to firmly entrench democratic principles and build a polity capable of delivering peace, reconciliation and reconstruction. The Hurriyat must, in this new phase, play a responsible role as a dissenting entity alongside the existing political parties, rather than as a spoiler standing outside the democratic framework.

CHAPTER 2: THE ARCHITECTURE OF TERROR

In this chapter, I move from the polling booth to the gun barrel. If the Introduction establishes that the people of Jammu and Kashmir were ready in 2002 to reclaim constitutional politics, this chapter explains why that choice was not enough to calm the Valley: the architecture of Pakistan-sponsored jihad remained intact, motivated, and externally sustained. Here, I dissect the ecosystem of terror that confronted India in 2002–2003. How organisations like Lashkar-e-Taiba and Jaish-e-Mohammed were raised, funded, trained and directed, and why any policy that treated them as mere by-products of local grievance was doomed to fail.

I begin by mapping the enemy as I saw it then: not an amorphous "anger on the streets" but a networked jihad project carefully constructed by Pakistan's military-intelligence establishment and its ideological partners. Lashkar and Jaish are examined not as faceless terror brands but as institutions with recruitment pipelines, command structures, social-welfare fronts and overseas funding channels. Their cadres did not spring spontaneously from Kashmir's soil; they flowed across the Line of Control, trained in camps protected by the Pakistani state, radicalised in seminaries, and shielded diplomatically by Islamabad under the fiction of a "freedom struggle". By 2002, a majority of violent incidents in Jammu and Kashmir were attributable to foreign militants, exposing the hollowness of claims that terrorism would fade once New Delhi made "political concessions".

The middle essays in this chapter use specific attacks–on Parliament, Akshardham, the Raghunath temple and other symbolic targets—to show how this architecture operated in practice. I analyse why jihadists repeatedly struck Parliament and major temples: not only to kill, but to send a message that no institution of Indian democracy or Hindu faith was beyond their reach. Each attack was both a tactical operation and strategic signalling from Rawalpindi: India would have to live with terror as a permanent condition, or accept negotiations on Pakistan's terms. Against this backdrop, I scrutinise the Mufti government's "healing touch" policy, arguing that well-meant gestures—releasing jailed militants en masse, lowering guard posts, and projecting softness—were read by Pakistan and its proxies as weakness, not magnanimity.

Towards the end of the chapter, I broaden the lens to make a larger argument about state-sponsored terrorism as a tool of weak but ambitious regimes. Drawing on examples from Russia-Chechnya, Sri Lanka-LTTE and beyond, I argue that when states allow or encourage non-state violence for strategic gain, they eventually lose control over the very forces they unleashed. In the Indian case, I contrast our own disastrous experiment with arming Tamil militants in Sri Lanka in the 1980s with Pakistan's far more sustained, and therefore far more dangerous, investment in jihadist groups operating in Afghanistan and Kashmir. I then step out further to examine the American push towards Iraq a decade after Operation Desert Storm, as a case study of a superpower trying to wrap a "war of choice" in the rhetoric of a war on terror—stretching non-proliferation regimes, sidelining the UN and fuelling precisely the polarisation it claimed to fear. The lesson I draw is simple but unfashionable at the time: terrorism is policy, not pathology; and a state that chooses it as an instrument will only change course when the costs, at home and abroad, become unacceptably high.

Taken together, the essays in Chapter 2 make three claims that are central to the rest of this book. First, by 2002-

2003, the primary driver of violence in Jammu and Kashmir was no longer local protest but an externally directed jihad machine under Pakistani patronage. Second, that any "peace process" which refused to confront this reality—by talking only of grievances and governance while ignoring training camps, infiltration routes and the wider global context of state-sponsored terror—was little more than theatre. Third, India's then-policy of strategic restraint, coupled with experiments in "soft separatism" at the state level, ensured that the enemy never believed there would be unbearable consequences for continuing to bleed us.

Seen from the vantage point of today—after Uri, Pulwama, the surgical strikes, Balakot and Operation Sindoor—this chapter reads almost as an indictment of the era before India decided to rewrite the rules. In 2002–2003, I was arguing that without a credible threat to the architecture of terror across the Line of Control, electoral successes in Kashmir would remain fragile and reversible. The country has since moved towards that harder line. Chapter 2 is my attempt to show, in the language and detail of that time, why it had to.

2.1 LASHKAR AND JAISH: PAKISTAN'S KILLING MACHINES IN KASHMIR

July 2002

The extended arms of the dreaded Al-Qaida in Pakistan and to its south (Pakistan-occupied Kashmir and Jammu and Kashmir) are Lashkar-e-Taiba. and Jaish-e-Mohammed. Both these ultra-fundamentalist groups are known to have had close ties with the former Taliban regime, and its downfall has been a tremendous setback for both outfits. A senior Indian analyst observes that Al-Qaida is increasingly likely to strengthen terrorist cadres in Pakistan and Pakistan-occupied Kashmir by coalescing with existing sub-groups and individuals, so that, regardless of the label, it is ultimately Al-Qaida that India will be fighting.

Jaish-e-Mohammed

Reports suggest that in Punjab (Pakistan) alone, the number of madrassas exceeds 2,500, with a similar number in the rest of the country. Of these, around 200 are controlled by the Ahl-e-Hadith sect and about 100 by the Shias, with the remainder roughly divided between the Barelvi and Deobandi schools of thought. Analysts point out that the grand Deobandi alliance is probably the most powerful force in Pakistan after the armed forces. Based in Karachi, the Banuri Complex houses leaders who sit in the shuras of Deobandi jehadi militias; Jaish-e-Mohammed and HuM (earlier HuA) are its militant wings.

It is reported that in 1979–80, about 100 Deobandi madrassas were selected for the Afghan war and provided military training by serving and retired Pakistan Army officers. The most important and active of these was the Jamiya Uloom-e-Islami at the Binori mosque in Karachi. Among the earliest "Army of Islam" recruits was Harkat-ul-Mujahideen, and an estimated three-quarters of HUM's members later defected to the newly formed Jaish-e-Mohammed. Most of Jaish-e-Mohammed's cadre and material resources have been drawn from HUJI and HUM, and the group has maintained close ties with Afghan Arabs and the Taliban, with Osama bin Laden widely believed to have funded it. Deobandi militias became powerful in part because the ISI ran Pakistan's Taliban policy. Jaish-e-Mohammed is currently headed by Maulana Masood Azhar, a former ultra-fundamentalist Harakat-ul-Ansar leader, who broke with his mentor, Maulana Fazlur-Rehman Khalil.

Lashkar-e-Taiba

Lashkar-e-Taiba is the armed wing of the Pakistan-based Sunni missionary organisation Markaz-ud-Dawa-wal-Irshad (MDI), founded in 1989. It is one of the three largest and best-trained groups fighting India in Kashmir and is not formally tied to a political party. Dawat-ul-Irshad is considered wealthy because of its strong grip on civil society in smaller districts, where it can effectively dictate terms to the local administration. Its leader, Hafiz Muhammad Saeed of the Gujjar community, was a retired Islamiyat teacher at the University of Engineering and Technology in Lahore. His headquarters complex at Muridke, often described as a "city within a city," was built with Arab funding; after the December 13 attack, he resigned under pressure and was replaced by Abdul Wahid Kashmiri, a foot soldier from Poonch.

Lashkar-e-Taiba's power also derives from its Salafi roots. Its contacts with Wahhabi training camps in Kunar, Afghanistan, have never been convincingly denied, even though Muridke publicly downplays links with Arab fighters. Its connections with Osama bin Laden have similarly been obfuscated, despite numerous press reports tying them together.

Terror Operations

Independent analysts now broadly confirm India's longstanding claim that over 70 per cent of the terrorists in Jammu and

Kashmir are foreign mercenaries, largely managed by Jaish-e-Mohammed and Lashkar-e-Taiba. Both organisations have been active in the Valley as well as the Poonch, Rajouri and Doda districts. Acting in coordination with Hizbul Mujahideen, Lashkar-e-Taiba has been instrumental in large-scale killings of minorities in south Kashmir (including Wandhama and later Chattisinghpora) and in the Doda region. Many of their cadres are veterans of the Afghan war, accustomed to treacherous terrain, and are known to take shelter in the higher ridges of the Pir Panjal range. Lashkar-e- Taiba has long been active in the Jammu region; because most of its cadres are Punjabi, they can easily blend with the local, linguistically related population. These groups have also inflicted heavy casualties on Indian security forces, and their fidayeen missions have sent chills through the local administration.

Jaish-e-Mohammed (then operating as Harkat) was instrumental in the hijacking of the Indian Airlines plane from Kathmandu to Kandahar to secure the release of its ideologue from an Indian prison. Its other spectacular operations include the October 1 attack on the Jammu and Kashmir state legislative assembly and the December 13 attack on the Indian Parliament, in coordination with allied groups. Gazi Baba, Jaish-e-Mohammed's chief operational commander in Kashmir, is believed to be from Bahawalpur in Pakistan and has been active in the Valley for nearly a decade, serving as the mastermind behind both the Assembly and Parliament attacks.

The post-December 13 scenario

Events following the December 13 Parliament attack have placed substantial pressure not only on these groups but also on their mentors in the ISI. Doubts, however, persist about the nature and sincerity of the Pakistani administration's actions. Islamabad insists that measures against Lashkar-e-Taiba and Jaish-e- Mohammed are aimed at their activities inside Pakistan. A State Bank of Pakistan spokesman, for instance, reportedly said he was unsure whether any Jaish accounts had actually been frozen, while the group itself claimed never to have held accounts in its own name, instead using those of office-bearers such as Mufti Rafeeq Ahmad. New Delhi has consistently argued that token arrests and asset-freezes are merely cosmetic steps designed to placate the international community. As one Indian columnist notes, those applauding cosmetic changes in Lashkar-e-Taiba and attributing them to Pakistani pressure miss the wood for the trees; they are, at best, "brownie points" for Pakistan, presented as evidence of a putative crackdown.

The real centre of gravity of Pakistan's terrorist infrastructure and command-and-control lies with the ISI–army combine, and no significant policy shift from Islamabad towards a genuine dismantling of jehadi outfits appears imminent. There are credible reports that Pakistan is restructuring the jihad machine: relabelling some parts to assuage demanding Western capitals while re-assembling others in Pakistan-occupied Kashmir, all aimed at enhancing "plausible deniability" ahead of future attacks. As commentator Rehan Ansari observes, Lashkars may be coordinated by the ISI, but they retain a will of their own. Pakistan-based mercenary groups such as Harkat, Jaish-e-Mohammed and Lashkar-e-Taiba have openly declared that they intend to expand their theatre of terrorist violence beyond Jammu and Kashmir to other parts of India.

Strategic analyst K. Subrahmanyam has neatly captured the complexity of Pakistan's internal situation, arguing that there is no way Pakistan can be "de- jihadised" unless it abandons the two-nation theory in its international relations. In his view, the two-nation theory mirrors the "clash of civilisations" thesis and is analogous to the Nazi Herrenvolk doctrine, while Pakistan's claim to Kashmir resembles Hitler's claims over German-speaking territories such as Austria, the Sudetenland and Danzig. On December 21, President

George W. Bush, addressing the financial underpinnings of terrorism, described Lashkar-e-Taiba as an extremist group "based in Kashmir," calling it a stateless sponsor of terror seeking to destroy India–Pakistan relations and undermine President Pervez Musharraf by committing attacks in both countries. Following Indian objections, the "based in Kashmir" formulation was quietly dropped, but the broader designation of Lashkar-e-Taiba as a global, rather than merely regional, terrorist threat was welcomed in New Delhi.

In recent days, there has been a visible tilt in Western attitudes towards India, with key capitals increasingly aligning with the Indian reading of cross-border terrorism. Analysts believe that, despite some differences in emphasis, there is emerging common ground that Pakistan must first acknowledge the depth of its malaise and demonstrate a clear determination to put its own house in order. In this context, New Delhi must fortify its position on Jammu and Kashmir and capitalise on the current diplomatic advantage to push the fight against Pakistan- sponsored terrorism towards a logical conclusion. What India must seek from Islamabad, as one political scientist on Kashmir affairs puts it, is a willingness to "back off" – to abandon its dream of annexing Kashmir and agree to live in peace.

New Delhi has already handed over to Pakistan a list of twenty terrorists and hardened criminals believed to be sheltering there, but, as expected, Islamabad's response, despite Western pressure, has been far from encouraging. Leading experts say the first real test will be whether India can secure strong international backing to ensure Pakistan's strict compliance with UN Security Council Resolution 1373 of 28 September 2001, including the handover of Masood Azhar and others for their role in the December 1999 hijacking of Indian Airlines flight IC-814 from Kathmandu to Kandahar.

2.2 AFTER AKSHARDHAM: ARE KASHI AND MATHURA NEXT?

October 2002

Two men believed to be associates of Lashkar-e-Taiba unleashed terror inside the Akshardham temple for about 12 hours, killing 36 and injuring over 70, in an attack that came seven months after the Godhra train tragedy - in which 60 Hindu pilgrims, including many women and children aboard the Sabarmati Express, were burnt alive by an unruly mob of Muslim fanatics - and the subsequent post-Godhra carnage. An attack bearing all the hallmarks of the earlier terrorist strikes on the Indian Parliament and the Jammu and Kashmir legislative assembly has once again sent shivers down the Indian establishment, which, despite tall claims, has been unable to curb the menace of terrorism.

No crime can be more culpable than the gratuitous killing of innocents engaged in worship. The massacre occurred despite several intelligence warnings, including a report following the Delhi Police's August discovery of a Lashkar-e-Taiba plot to assassinate Chief Minister Narendra Modi, VHP leader Praveen Togadia and other Sangh figures. Super-cop K. P. S. Gill had also warned that terrorist strikes in Gujarat were likely, but his timely assessment went unheeded, with the state intelligence and police forces caught napping.

Having failed in its design to derail the election process in Jammu and Kashmir, the terrorist network then trained its guns on Gujarat to "retaliate" for the post-Godhra killings of Muslims. New Delhi is firmly convinced that this latest outrage is the handiwork of Pakistan, rattled by the high turnout in the first three phases of the Jammu and Kashmir Assembly polls. The shameful attack on Hindu devotees is unquestionably a Pakistan-inspired and Pakistan-executed terrorist operation, coming just weeks after President Pervez

Musharraf raised the Gujarat issue at the United Nations to accuse the Indian government of a supposed "Hindu bias."

Given the quantity and type of ammunition carried by the two gunmen, they appear to have been well-trained and are believed to be members of Lashkar-e- Taiba. The Gujarat riots, media reports suggest, provided fresh fodder to Lashkar chief Hafiz Saeed, who has invoked them repeatedly in his speeches following the crackdown in Pakistan and has reportedly urged his cadres to move south to seek revenge. Intelligence analysts are convinced that the weapons and tactics used at Akshardham point squarely to Lashkar's suicide squads. Jaish-e-Mohammed, led by Maulana Masood Azhar - himself of Gujarati origin on the other side of the border - is also under suspicion, with highly placed sources in New Delhi suggesting that while the modus operandi was Lashkar-style, the foot soldiers could have come from Jaish.

Following the Akshardham attack, the Uttar Pradesh government, acting on Home Ministry advice, rushed additional police and paramilitary forces to Ayodhya, Kashi and Mathura - three major holy towns in the state - to foil any fidayeen attempts. In a pattern visible since the early 1980s, when scores of temples were desecrated in Kashmir, the focus has now shifted to other parts of India, with Hindu temples being targeted and devotees gunned down in cold blood. The attack on the famous Raghunath temple in Jammu and a series of attacks on the annual holy Amarnath pilgrimage in Kashmir have confirmed what was already obvious: jihadi forces, under firm instructions from their controllers in the ISI, have been tasked with mounting sensational attacks on sacred Hindu sites.

According to a credible report with the National Human Rights Commission (NHRC), militants damaged 127 temples in the Valley between 1986 and 1992, including 32 temples destroyed within 48 hours of the demolition of the disputed structure at Ayodhya on 6 December 1992. The report notes that a maximum of 47 temples were vandalised and damaged in February 1986, followed by 44 in 1992; of these, 72 temples were vandalised in Anantnag, the rest in Srinagar, Baramulla, Kupwara, Badgam and Shopian. The report further confirms that temple lands were usurped, idols were damaged by explosions, and many shrines were destroyed in rocket and grenade attacks.

With resolute backing from Islamabad, jihadi forces are expected to persist in their campaign against Hinduism by selectively targeting key Hindu holy places across the length and breadth of the country. New Delhi, meanwhile, must do far more than offer the poetic rhetoric of Prime Minister Vajpayee in an attempt to placate the majority community. Even after enacting tough legislation such as POTA, India has failed to curb the terrorist threat, which, instead of receding, is spreading to fresh parts of the country. By failing to safeguard the lives of its citizens, the NDA government at the Centre has made India a laughing stock in the eyes of the world, rushing to "Uncle Sam" for assistance every time an atrocity occurs.

In stark contrast to India's rhetoric, Washington avenged the killing of over 7,000 people in the World Trade Centre and Pentagon attacks through swift, decisive action in Afghanistan that toppled the Taliban and put Al-Qaida to flight. New Delhi, by comparison, has been unable even to apprehend the prime accused in the Bombay serial blasts, let, alone the terrorists responsible for hijacking the IC-814 Indian Airlines flight.

It is time for India to abandon mere rhetoric; confront Pakistan with all its might and make it clear to the international community that this country is fully capable of crippling the nerve-centres of terrorism on its own. India must signal that it will not rest until Pakistan halts the cross-border jihad it has unleashed. The minority community in India, too, must honestly confront a fundamental question: why is it that one community alone repeatedly acquires the global notoriety of being associated with terrorism?

2.3 DO WE NEED HINDU SUICIDE SQUADS IN RESPONSE?

November 2002

Shiv Sena supremo Bal Thackeray has created a hullabaloo of sorts - not that the phenomenon is new - by urging Hindus to form suicide squads to battle the growing menace of terrorism in the country. The million-dollar question is what impelled him to issue such a diktat, given that his own party is an important component of the BJP-led government in New Delhi. His remarks, one could argue, reflect the growing frustration of the majority community, which, in the wake of a series of attacks first in Jammu and Kashmir and now in other parts of the country, feels increasingly apprehensive despite having accepted a secular dispensation to accommodate the aspirations of minority communities.

The most charitable reading of his assertion runs as follows: if the ISI, Pakistan's disreputable intelligence arm, can use right-wing jihadi elements to foment trouble in India, why cannot Indian intelligence, RAW, employ right-wing Hindu elements to respond in kind? A second strand of this argument is that if jihadi groups can form suicide squads with the full backing of the junta in Pakistan and unleash a reign of terror in India by killing Hindus, what prevents our establishment from reciprocating with similar methods?

The wider family of right-wing Hindu organisations has shown little enthusiasm for these propositions. The RSS, ideological mentor of the ruling BJP, has candidly rejected the idea, arguing that such tactics run counter to the tenets of Hinduism and therefore cannot be put into practice. The broader logic behind the "use-their-methods" argument has, however, long existed in another form - the contention that weakening Pakistan as a state by supporting its disgruntled elements would benefit India. This thesis was implemented to the point of success in the separation of East Pakistan, where RAW played an instrumental role. Imagine the strategic nightmare India would face today if East Pakistan had remained part of Pakistan; incidentally, contrary to common assumptions, India's longest land border today is with Bangladesh, not Pakistan.

Yet, given the changed world order, repeating the Bangladesh model is neither feasible nor desirable. In The Pakistan Papers, Mani Shankar Aiyar discusses four major approaches to dealing with Pakistan, one of which is to explore ways of bringing about its balkanisation. He immediately undercuts the idea, however, noting that such an outcome may not serve India's long-term interests and, in any case, India lacks the requisite leverage within Pakistan to execute so radical a plan. Pakistan itself has long used its state machinery to try to sever Kashmir from India by waging a low-intensity proxy war with the help of disaffected elements in the Valley, yet it has clearly failed to achieve its objective, raising serious doubts about the viability of such strategies. At the same time, India must accept blame for its own dismal record in repeatedly subverting democratic principles in Kashmir by using state power to rig elections for partisan advantage. Pakistan's emotional investment in the Kashmir issue, moreover, springs in large measure from its desire to avenge the loss of East Pakistan and the creation of Bangladesh.

There is broad agreement that terrorism exported from Islamabad must be countered effectively. The mechanism for counter-action, however, cannot involve reducing ourselves to the level of those who openly sponsor terrorism. India is a democratic polity known worldwide for its values and principles, and it cannot afford to be seen dabbling in terrorism of any hue. Even if we were able to recruit disgruntled Pakistanis - and such elements certainly exist - it would not help India reduce violence at home and could very well deepen the chaos. Proponents of "reciprocating in kind" argue that raising the costs for Pakistan and destabilising it fits neatly into India's strategic toolkit. This is loose talk from people unwilling to confront ground realities in Pakistan: the more pressure you apply in this manner, the likelier you are to push Pakistan into an Afghanistan-style meltdown, with hard-core fundamentalists at the helm who might not hesitate to plunge South Asia into a nuclear holocaust.

There is, therefore, an urgent need to re-examine India's internal security environment and confront the growing presence of ISI cells on our soil, but the fantasy of balkanising Pakistan by exporting "our" brand of terrorism in the form of Hindu suicide squads should be laid to rest once and for all. India need not engage in low-intensity proxy warfare; if Pakistan has behaved badly, India is under no obligation to respond in an even worse fashion. New Delhi enjoys a clear edge in conventional military power and, should the need arise, is fully capable of taking the fight into enemy territory like a self-respecting nation, rather than behaving like cowards who go on killing sprees simply because people belong to a different nationality or faith.

One so-called expert based in the United States has argued in a recent paper that if India fails to shed its "negative" image, thanks to its mantra of restraint, and continues on the same path, it is destined to be balkanised, with each fragment paraded as "Islam's latest conquest." Such pessimistic overdrive about one's own country is misplaced. What India does need, urgently, is to initiate serious pre-emptive action against terrorist camps across the Line of Control to demonstrate to Pakistan that we are not cowed by nuclear threats and will not hesitate to unleash legitimate military force if it does not halt its covert activities in Kashmir and other parts of India.

2.4 MUFTI'S 'HEALING TOUCH': RIGHT TRACK OR ILLUSION?

December 2002

The PDP-led coalition government in Jammu and Kashmir will have to wake up to pragmatism sooner rather than later. The false sense of security into which it had lulled itself has been shattered in less than 48 hours, in rapid succession: first the attack on the CRPF barracks in the heart of Srinagar; second, the IED explosion on the strategic Jammu–Srinagar national highway, killing army personnel and their families; and then the ruthless suicide attack on the symbolic and historic Raghunath temple, taking a heavy toll of human life. This is the second such attack on this sacred place of worship, and early reports indicate largely civilian casualties. No crime can be more culpable than the gratuitous killing of innocents engaged in worship. It was not long ago that Lashkar-e-Toiba (Lashkar-e-Taiba) wrought terror inside the Akshardham temple in Gujarat for about 12 hours, killing 36 and injuring over 70 worshippers.

These suicide attacks have come within days of Islamabad's decision to release Hafiz Saeed, the Lashkar-e-Taiba chief, despite reservations expressed by its partner in the "war on terror", the United States. His release has undoubtedly rejuvenated the sagging morale of cadres operating in Jammu and Kashmir, and Lashkar-e-Taiba will almost certainly step up its activities in the state. Given the quantity and type of ammunition carried by the attackers, they appear well-trained and are believed to be Lashkar-e-Taiba members. Media reports suggest that the Gujarat unrest provided fresh fodder for Hafiz Saeed, who has repeatedly used it in his speeches following the crackdown in Pakistan and has reportedly urged his cadres to "move south" to seek revenge. Intelligence analysts are convinced that the weapons and strategy in the Raghunath temple attack point squarely to Lashkar's suicide squads.

Chief Minister Mufti Mohammad Sayeed, a deft politician in his own right, has adroitly touched the "acupuncture points" of Kashmiri sentiment to revive his political fortunes. Passions have a populist edge and politicians go where passions catch fire, so it is hardly surprising that he now talks in terms of "healing touch", "unconditional dialogue", "sensitive and humane government" and "peace with dignity and honour". He has geared up the state machinery to present a sharp contrast to the freewheeling style of Farooq Abdullah's government. Yet by casting himself as a dream merchant, Mufti has placed himself in a knotty position, and extricating himself from the expectations he has created will be no easy task.

With the emotional tide in the Valley somewhat receding, it is time for sober reflection. Many observers believe the PDP now stands at a threshold between mainstream politics and political separatism, tempted to straddle two boats at once - one representing democratic aspirations and the other flirting with secessionist sentiment. A more realistic assessment, however, is that the passions crafted by Sayeed will do little to end the menace of terrorism. He appears to turn a blind eye to the overarching threat from Pakistan, as if it did not exist. Much remains to be seen as to whether separatist elements in the Valley will firmly board the "peace train" he has flagged off.

The coalition's blueprint for a "sensitive and humane government" as a means of ending bloodshed in Jammu and Kashmir has not met with wide acceptance in analytical and security circles, where serious doubts are voiced about its efficacy. Given the ground realities, the paramount issues are the sustained attacks by radical Islamist forces, through their militant wings Jaish-e- Mohammed and Lashkar-e-Taiba (which account for roughly 70 per cent of the violence), on security personnel and innocent civilians. The coalition should focus its energies on these pressing threats; debates over autonomy or self-determination can wait. As one analyst aptly notes, these foreign mercenaries "operate beyond the reach of a healing touch".

In this context, the PDP-led government's decision to wind up the controversial Special Operations Group (SOG) under the guise of "assimilation or reallocation within Jammu and Kashmir Police" may, in time, prove unwise, given SOG's instrumental role in fighting cross-border terrorism for over a decade and a half. For now, SOG personnel can take solace in the words of Julio Ribeiro, who, as Punjab DGP at the height of militancy, said that if someone tried to kill him or his men, and that person was an armed terrorist, they would "get him first". It is imperative that the PDP government first devise robust ways and means of tackling Pakistan-sponsored militancy before dismantling one of its key counter-terrorist instruments.

As part of the coalition's effort to give detainees a "fair trial", top militant commanders from earlier phases of the insurgency are being bailed out under a major policy shift. Contrary to what Sayeed appears to have expected, the separatists - led by Yasin Malik - have fired the first salvo, challenging the chief minister to prove that he is the "true representative" of the people by contesting a seat from the Valley. This will come as a shock to PDP's rank and file, who were assured of a conciliatory approach by the Hurriyat Conference. The manner in which these separatist figures have been freed casts serious doubt on the functioning of the judiciary, which, until the other day, seemed to have adequate evidence to hold them, but has suddenly discovered that there is nothing to incriminate them.

These gestures by the PDP government must not send the wrong signals to Pakistan-sponsored militants, who may be tempted to interpret them as sympathetic or supportive. The situation is uncomfortably reminiscent of Punjab where, after Operation Bluestar, terrorism briefly subsided before resurfacing when a popular Akali government opened political space and communication channels that militants exploited. The PDP must ensure such mistakes are not repeated; otherwise, the Valley could slide back to the chaos and pandemonium of 1990. Fears of unintended consequences are both real and justified. Talk of turning Kashmir into a "bridge" between India and Pakistan and insisting on Pakistan's inclusion in every dialogue process sounds dangerously naïve and simplistic.

Another contentious move is the government's decision to dispense with the Prevention of Terrorism Act (POTA) on the premise that enough laws already exist to deal with militancy. Experts argue that POTA is the only instrument that criminalises the mobilisation and transfer of financial resources to terrorists in India. Militants have repeatedly been caught with large sums of money earmarked for funding the insurgency in the Valley, and Section 22 of POTA uniquely provides for stricter procedures and penalties in such cases. Without such provisions, anti-militancy operations risk being seriously hamstrung.

Mufti Sayeed has himself witnessed the entire arc of Kashmir's recent turmoil and transformation, and he has executed a sharp U-turn in terms of ideological posture. Many still view him as the "muscle" who helped unleash state terror in the Valley a decade and a half ago, and his critics accuse him of using the present opportunity to further his political fortunes. One of his gravest misjudgements was the release of five militants in exchange for his daughter, Rubaiya Sayeed, in 1989, when he was Union Home Minister, against the advice of the then ruling NC and central intelligence officials who were confident the JKLF would have freed her under public pressure. He played a key role in dismissing the NC government in February 1990 and is widely believed to have been pivotal in the appointment of Jagmohan as governor –

and the rest is grim history.

Burdened with this chequered record, Sayeed appears determined not to take chances this time and has plunged into an overdrive to engineer a "transition" in the Valley without any corresponding change in Pakistan-sponsored militancy on the ground. Committing to "unconditional dialogue" with everyone, before fully weighing the implications, seems flippant and naïve and raises serious questions about the future of counter-terror operations in Jammu and Kashmir. And, last but not least, a word of counsel for Mufti Sahib, from one wise man to another: any kind of compromise is not necessarily better than no solution at all.

2.4 WORLD-JUNGLE: BUSHFIRE SPREADS TO IRAQ

November 2002

It has been ten years since Operation Desert Storm, a campaign that left what many Americans see as a "messed-up outcome". Renewed efforts are now evident in Washington to push its agenda into overdrive against Iraq, a country that holds the world's second-largest proven oil reserves - roughly one-fifth of global supply. Iraq has been rebranded over time from a "rogue state" to a charter member of the "axis of evil" in American parlance, and critics argue that US policy is aimed as much at controlling those oil taps - turning them off or on at will - as at any security concern.

Long-standing critics of American strategy warn of dire consequences if Washington continues to act with a "Cold War posture" in a post-Cold War world, noting that in East Asia and Central America, it often behaves no better than the communist bureaucrats it opposed. History shows that domestic ideals have rarely restrained US interventions in Latin America or the Philippines, and with Iraq, the United States appears intent on staying an imperial course. Despite repeated attempts, it has still not removed Saddam Hussein, and analysts suggest that surviving Iraqis are likely to harbour deep resentment against both the US government and its citizens.

The reported insertion of CIA paramilitary operatives into UN weapons-inspection teams is widely seen as having tainted one of the most promising experiments in non-proliferation verification. Former US intelligence analyst Kenneth M. Pollack, in The Threatening Storm, estimates that Baghdad's chemical and biological arsenals are relatively small, its missile inventory limited to a handful of short-range systems, and its nuclear ambitions still several years away - a picture that makes the US case for urgent war look decidedly weak. Many observers also note that the 1991 Gulf War was a catalytic event for Islamist radicals who went on to form Al Qaeda, and fear that another conflict could further radicalise the region.

Foreign-policy experts warn that an assault on Iraq risks polarising the world order into Islamic and non-Islamic blocs, with consequences that would echo for generations. The more Washington sets itself against the rest of the world, they argue, the greater the temptation for adversaries to adopt unconventional means - from terrorism to cyber-attacks - aided by new technologies. Combined with the aggressive style associated with President Bush's Texan background and the triumphalist tone of US economic success, this posture may be creating more enemies than America can handle.

America's declared ambition appears to be to entrench its dominance indefinitely, yet history is replete with examples of overextended empires collapsing under their own weight. Washington has repeatedly sidelined or strong-armed the United Nations when it suited its purposes, even while a serial defaulter on its own UN dues, leading one scholar to remark that a government which has often placed US law above international obligations now demands that the UN "grow a spine" to serve American ends. After 9/11, a profound sense of vulnerability fused with unrivalled power, pushing the US towards a project of reshaping the world, beginning with West Asia. Even sympathetic analysts concede that Iraq represents a "war of choice", not necessity, and caution that any regional convulsions are unlikely to yield lasting benefits for either American or Israeli security.

Reliable reports from Washington suggest that the administration underestimates the chaos a new Desert Storm could unleash, while overestimating its own capacity to turn regime change into a stable, democratic and

US-friendly Iraq. There are serious doubts about America's staying power for post-war reconstruction; many fear a Kabul-style arrangement in Baghdad that will lack legitimacy and sow the seeds of further turmoil. Hence the insistence by many analysts that any action be channelled through the UN, with post-conflict nation-building conducted under multilateral auspices as in Bosnia rather than dominated by Washington as in Beirut.

Saddam Hussein is rightly viewed as a brutal ruler with terrible weapons and an unpardonable record, including the invasion and annexation of Kuwait. Yet equating him with Osama bin Laden stretches credibility; Iraq has certainly backed terrorism in the past, but largely of the traditional, state-sponsored variety. Supporters of US policy counter that the UN "oil-for-food" programme has strengthened Saddam by giving him control over lucrative contracts and revenue streams, which he can divert into weapons programmes while blaming sanctions for Iraqi suffering. Independent estimates, however, suggest that the sanctions regime from 1991 to the late 1990s contributed to hundreds of thousands of civilian deaths through disease, malnutrition and collapsed public services, a catastrophe various UN bodies have documented.

Initial US claims about Iraqi weapons of mass destruction and the much-touted British dossier have failed to convince many governments, prompting Washington to pivot towards alleging links between Baghdad and Al Qaeda. President George W. Bush has declared that the two are "equally evil" and indistinguishable in the war on terror, but most regional experts argue that Iraq's secular Ba'athist regime and Al Qaeda's jihadist ideology are natural enemies. For Al Qaeda, secular Muslim rulers who refuse to govern by strict Islamic law are traitors, and the United States is targeted as their principal external sponsor. While there is some concern that a cornered Saddam might seek tactical cooperation with Al Qaeda in a last-ditch gamble, the evidence so far does not support treating Iraq as a seamless extension of the anti-terror campaign.

In reality, a more sober appraisal of the tenuous and largely adversarial relationship between Saddam's regime and Al Qaeda weakens the case for an immediate war on Iraq and strengthens the argument for focusing first on dismantling Al Qaeda's global network. Far from being a logical continuation of the war on terror, an invasion of Iraq risks diverting attention and resources, inflaming grievances across the Muslim world and undermining precisely the international cooperation needed to confront transnational jihadist movements.

CHAPTER 3: PAKISTAN'S INSTABILITY AND GEOPOLITICS

In Chapter 3, I argue that the violence in Jammu and Kashmir by 2002–2003 was driven primarily by an externally sustained jihad machine. In this chapter, I turn the lens across the Line of Control and ask a blunt question: what kind of state needs terrorism as an instrument of policy? My answer, developed through these essays, is that Pakistan's internal fragility, its unresolved identity crisis and its military–mullah nexus made the export of jihad to Kashmir and beyond not a temporary tactic but an almost structural compulsion.

I start by laying out what I then called Pakistan's "unstable core". Decades of alternating between military rule and flawed civilian experiments had produced a polity where no durable consensus existed beyond Islam, and even Islam itself was fractured into competing Deobandi, Barelvi, Wahhabi and Shia currents. The army had become, as observers like V.S. Naipaul and Pakistani scholars themselves noted, a "country within a country"—the only fully organised institution, using religion first as a source of legitimacy and then as a tool of mobilisation. In this environment, generals like Zia-ul-Haq and Musharraf did not accidentally stumble into an alliance with clerics; they built and funded an entire jihad infrastructure, from madrassa networks to proxy militias, that could be pointed outward at Afghanistan and Kashmir whenever domestic pressures rose.

The essays that follow trace how this theo-military compact played out in the early 2000s. I examine General Musharraf's post-January 12, 2002 "reforms", his Legal

Framework Order and the carefully managed elections that produced a pliant civilian façade under Prime Minister Zafarullah Khan Jamali. Behind the theatrics, the real levers of power—national security, Kashmir policy, nuclear decision-making—remained firmly in GHQ Rawalpindi. I describe Jamali as "old wine in a new bottle" because his primary function was to give Washington and the international community a talking face while the army entrenched its constitutional supremacy through institutions like the National Security Council.

At the same time, Pakistan's religious parties were not receding; they were resurgent. The rise of the Muttahida Majlis-e-Amal (MMA)—an alliance of six Islamist parties—to unprecedented strength in the 2002 elections signalled that anti-American sentiment and fundamentalist ideology had acquired an electoral base, particularly in the provinces bordering Afghanistan. In my reading, the MMA's success did three things. It legitimised the very forces that had fed the Afghan jihad and later the Kashmir insurgency; it gave Musharraf an alibi to resist Western pressure on terror camps by pointing to his "difficult domestic constituency"; and it increased the risk that sections of the army itself would be ideologically captured by the religious right.

From there, I widen the frame to Bangladesh, which I describe as Pakistan's "alter ego". Drawing parallels between the erosion of secular Bengali nationalism and the rise of Jamaat-e-Islami and allied groups in Dhaka, I argue that the same model—military and intelligence agencies patronising Islamist outfits, madrassa proliferation, and permissive attitudes toward terrorist training—was taking root on India's eastern flank. Organisations like HUJI-Bangladesh, with reported arms camps and documented links to ISI and Kashmir-focused groups, turned Bangladesh into a secondary staging ground for jihad against India. The point I make is uncomfortable but necessary: by the early 2000s, India faced not just a western front of state-sponsored jihad from Pakistan, but a slowly emerging eastern one as well.

The final set of essays in this chapter takes on the United States and the wider West. I describe Washington's posture as "double speak" because, while loudly proclaiming a global "War on Terror", it continued to treat Pakistan as an indispensable ally, funnelling money and arms into a state that was simultaneously harbouring, tolerating, or selectively targeting the very networks the US claimed to fight. I note how American officials praised Bangladesh's "commitment to combating terrorism" even as evidence mounted of Islamist consolidation there, and how US policy consistently viewed India through the prism of Pakistan's utility in Afghanistan. My critique is not anti-American in a reflexive sense; it is a strategic warning that indulgence toward Pakistan's jihad infrastructure in the 1980s and 1990s had created a monster, and that post-9/11 half-measures would not easily unwind it.

Put simply, Chapter 3 makes four linked arguments. First, that Pakistan's reliance on religious extremism and proxies is rooted in its unresolved nationhood and army-centric power structure, not in any particular Indian action in Kashmir. Second, that the rise of the MMA and the spread of jihadist influence into Bangladesh showed this was a regional project, not an isolated aberration. Third, that Western leniency—born of short-term strategic needs in Afghanistan—allowed Pakistan to keep its anti-India terror apparatus largely intact. And fourth, that as long as this structural problem remained unaddressed, any Indian policy based solely on "dialogue" and "confidence-building" would be operating on a dangerously false premise.

Seen from today's vantage point, after years of cross-border attacks, nuclear brinkmanship and finally India's shift to a more assertive doctrine culminating in Balakot and Operation Sindoor, the logic of this chapter is even clearer. If Chapter 2 explains the mechanics of the gunman who crosses the Line of Control, Chapter 3 explains the unstable state and the indulgent international environment that keep sending him. Together, they build the case for why India eventually had to move beyond restraint and why any serious discussion on Kashmir that ignores Pakistan's internal deformities will always be strategically naïve.

3.1 PAKISTAN: THE STARK REALITIES

June 2002

During the American Revolution, when the work of the courts was disrupted, a public-spirited citizen called Charles Lynch took charge of law and order as an unofficial justice of the peace in Bedford County, Virginia. General Musharraf, the self-proclaimed junta ruler of Pakistan, in his post-January 12 speech has assumed the role of "Lynch law" enforcer, set out to initiate remedial measures to bring order to Pakistani society, a task of gigantic and Herculean proportions. For a state that has experienced 24 years of military rule in 52 years of nationhood, the process of transition from a radical Islamic state to a "progressive democratic republic" will not be an easy one.

The law-and-order situation in Pakistan has been in a state of anarchy and pandemonium, a problem that emerged and evolved out of the theo-fascist tendencies of Pakistani rulers, who have over a period of time experimented with various forms of governance, largely at the expense of their own people. Says Pratap Mehta, Professor at JNU, "Pakistan was, during much of the last two decades, in the impossible situation that it could neither endure its condition, nor the means of changing it. It tried everything to no avail: authoritarian rule, democracy, religious fundamentalism and military dictatorship."

Pakistan, unlike India, does not have equal dispensation of power amongst its ethnic population, a factor that has been responsible for the growing resentment among sections of society who feel marginalised in the day-to-day affairs of the country. Mani Shankar Aiyar, in his book Pakistan Papers, writes, "Pakistan after separation of East Pakistan may be geographically more cohesive than the Pakistan of yore, but all the other fissiparous forces remain: language and culture divide the Punjabi from the Sindhi; the Baluch from the Pathan, and equally each of them from the other; the vexed question of a unitary or a federal or a confederal constitution runs like a rift valley through the polity of the country."

The ethnic and religious schism within Pakistan threatens the cohesiveness (single religion) that has been the basis of the formation of Pakistan. Says a former Indian diplomat, "The votaries of Islamic Pakistan are pitted against those who say a Pakistani may be a Muslim but a Muslim's relations with God are no concern of the state; worse, those who want an Islamic state bitterly fight each other about which school of Islam - the Wahabi or the Brehelvi or the Deobandi... The nationhood of Pakistan remains as elusive a chimera as it ever was."

The social and political reach of the theo-fascist forces in Pakistan has scaled new heights with the aid of state sponsorship. Professor K. N. Pandita, a known strategic analyst, believes that these forces have ideologically integrated with their counterparts in the Islamic world and also with the strong Muslim diaspora in the West. He says, "Pakistan is wearing alternatively the mask of democracy, martial law administration or theocratic dispensation. She is a moderate Islamic democracy to the West, a staunch Sunni-Wahabi pro-monarchy theocracy to the Saudis, a progressive, liberal and scientific Muslim state to the Central Asians, the only sympathetic fraternity to the Indian Muslims, and the milk-and-honey-flowing cherished haven for the Kashmiri Muslims." Pakistan seeks to identify itself with West Asia and knowingly undermines the significance of the subcontinent as a strategic entity.

Pakistan, over the years, has clearly demonstrated its inability to set itself free from the quagmire of fundamentalist tendencies, a factor responsible for the rise of militant activities in Pakistan. Commenting on the sorry state of affairs in his country, a Pakistani columnist in his article "A City Without Leadership" in The Nation says, "The ethnic and religious schisms have still not been successfully exploited by those interested in Pakistan's destruction but they can be unless we bind ourselves together and create conditions where terrorism can never be nurtured let alone have places of sanctuary to operate from. Only sound, mature governance that must equally exploit both the carrot and the stick can create a conducive environment that will allow the citizens of this city to breathe the Pakistani air with freedom."

A state like Pakistan is characterised by an overriding concern with domestic security threats and by insufficient political and societal consensus to enable it to eliminate the large-scale use of force. Nobel laureate V. S. Naipaul, in his book Among the Believers, throws light on the dominant role of the army in the domestic affairs of Pakistan. He observes, "In the new state, only the armed forces flourished. They were seen first as defenders, and possible extenders, of the Islamic state. Then it became apparent that they were the state's only organised group. They became masters, a country within a country. The armed forces were mainly of the Northwest, with the cultural prejudices of the Northwest; in time, they found they forced the eastern wing of Pakistan into secession as Bangladesh."

We must also recognise that Pakistan will accommodate itself to the wishes of its external benefactors because it is too small and unimportant to be truly non-aligned. Uncle Sam has played a significant role in transforming Pakistan into a radical Islamic state, primarily to safeguard its interests in the region. Says Dr Parvez Hoodbhoy of Quaid-e-Azam University, "The lack of scruple and the pursuit of power by the United States combined fatally with this tide in Muslim world in 1979, when the Soviet Union invaded Afghanistan. Radical Islam went into overdrive as its superpower ally and mentor funneled support to the mujahadeen."

The costs and consequences of American imperialistic

tendencies have been articulated by Chalmers Johnson, a known critic of American foreign policy, in his critically acclaimed book Blowback. He observes, "The bombing of Afghanistan will certainly produce unintended negative consequences throughout the Islamic and underdeveloped worlds. Moderate Muslim governments, especially in Saudi Arabia, Egypt and Pakistan, will almost certainly face growing internal dissent and may be overthrown. America has played its role by funneling money through ISI, which has taken lead since 1982 in recruiting the radical Muslims to come to Pakistan, receive training, and fight on the Afghanistan side in its fight against the erstwhile USSR."

Doubtless India and Pakistan are separate geographical entities. But then, is it fair to undermine the legacy of their shared past and collective memories? On the contrary, many in India, according to a senior analyst, feel that anti-Indianism is so much at the core of Pakistan's identity that it is difficult to imagine that anti-India sentiments will not reassert themselves there after a while.

Many in India believe that Pakistan will have to undergo a radical transformation as a result of the war against terrorism. The reform process initiated by General Pervez Musharraf, in the opinion of many analysts, will require support from the Indian establishment, something that is not forthcoming in the present scenario. The former chief of the Intelligence Bureau, M. K. Narayanan, says, "Musharraf's sleight-of-hand policies are seen as a manifest attempt by a Muslim leader to posit a real challenge to the radical political Islam, one that goes well beyond merely regulating mosques and madrassas and one that deserves to be fully backed." The Indian establishment also has to come to terms with the ground realities; a senior strategic analyst says, "A weak and self-doubting Pakistan is trouble for us and it is dangerous to harbour the illusion, which many in India share, that Pakistan can somehow be broken up."

General Musharraf spent seven years of his childhood in Turkey - one of the world's most secularised Muslim countries - and is known to have learned to speak Turkish. So it is not much of a surprise that the General seeks to take a leaf out of Kemal Atatürk's book in separating mosque and state. He has the additional advantage of having the backing of Uncle Sam and the rest of the international community. Musharraf has the distinction of being the first leader of Pakistan who has followed in the footsteps of the founder of Pakistan.

However, his critics see him as the architect of Kargil and the man who rubbished the Lahore Declaration. Many in India believe that the General has been clever enough to create fresh space for himself to manoeuvre - an Indian rope-trick on India. The General has received accolades, especially from the international community, for his decision to withdraw state sponsorship of militant Islamists. However, many feel that there is an urgent need for a stable political framework, something that is unlikely to emerge if, through administrative manoeuvres, key segments of Pakistani society continue to be excluded from the power structure.

Husain Haqqani, who has served both Benazir Bhutto and Nawaz Sharif, believes that the process of reforms in Pakistan is incomplete without a process that will ensure a free judiciary, a non-political civil service and a non-interfering military.

In his paper titled Pakistan's Madrassas: Ensuring a System of Education not Jehad, P. W. Singer, foreign-policy studies fellow at the Brookings Institution, says that any direct operation against the schools themselves could undermine the military's unity and hence its role as a bulwark of the secular Pakistani state. He further observes: "Even if [the] Pakistani government was willing to make such an aggressive step at this time of tension, any such direct move against the schools could potentially backfire and hasten the collapse of the Pakistani state." Many will argue that the paper has gone into a pessimistic over-drive, but one thing is certain: Pakistan has to be "purged of fundamentalism just as Germany was denazified and Japan was demilitarized.

3.2 PAKISTAN: IN A CORNER

June 2002

Since the inception of the decade-long militancy in Kashmir, aided and abetted by Pakistan, this is the first time there has been unequivocal and overwhelming support for India in the international community against the growing menace of Islamic fundamentalism in particular and cross-border terrorism in general.

The international community, led by the Western democracies, has openly endorsed India's viewpoint, much to the dismay of its so-called ally in the war against global terrorism. Statements from all quarters indicate that the world has come to realise that Pakistan itself is the hub and nerve centre of Islamic terrorism, and that General Musharraf has betrayed the cause of fighting global terrorism by failing to translate words into action, remaining a mute spectator to the activities of Islamic groups targeting Indian establishments across the Line of Control.

In a highly charged atmosphere, Pakistan feels cornered by India's conventional military might and has openly resorted to nuclear threats despite India's commitment to "no first use". Pakistan's latest threats are part of a game plan to placate its domestic constituency, but in doing so it has irked Western democracies to such an extent that it has pushed itself into a deeper quagmire. General Musharraf now finds his support base dwindling at home and abroad, a sign many analysts believe weakens him so much that his regime could be toppled by one of his own trusted lieutenants, possibly with CIA support.

Such hostile postures have not gone down well with Western democracies and, given that there has been no meaningful de-escalation, the US and UK have advised their citizens to pull out of India and Pakistan as soon as possible. Sundeep Waslekar, an expert in conflict resolution, argues in a recent report on Pakistan that jihadi elements are fast emerging as the "voice of conscience" there and may prey not only on popular frustrations but also on sympathetic corps commanders within the Pakistan army.

Although hectic behind-the-scenes parleys continue in politico-diplomatic circles to de-escalate the stand-off, highly placed sources indicate a growing rift between Secretary of State Colin Powell and President Musharraf after the latter's recent speech. Pakistan's move to pull back forces from the Afghan border leaves American troops more vulnerable in their operations against the Taliban, something Washington bitterly resents.

It is imperative that pressure on Pakistan is not relaxed until it takes concrete measures to eradicate the roots of Islamic fundamentalism and stops its proxy war against India. If Pakistan refuses to heed the genuine concerns of India in particular and the international community in general, full economic sanctions on the lines of those imposed on Iraq should follow. In the event that Islamabad defies its commitments in the war on terror, India should be fully backed to take whatever steps it deems necessary to safeguard its national interests.

3.3 PAKISTAN: 'MILITARY-MOSQUE' NEXUS REJUVENATED

November 2002

Since independence in 1947, Pakistan has oscillated between civilian and military rule in an endless series of coup d'états, eliminations and regime firings. Frail political institutions and a failing economy have added to its multifaceted crisis. The tribulations are largely internal, and the grave task of initiating remedial measures will also have to be internal. Pakistan's domestic problems are a complex coalescence of political, economic and social concerns, and the fact that it has historically had thorny relationships with two of its neighbours completes the grim picture. The health of Pakistan's political institutions is further undermined by limitations in its legal system. In the post-September 11 scenario, it is apparent that Pakistan's conduct of foreign policy is inseparable from its domestic policy. The intricate correlation between Islam, Pakistan and its people is central to most of these problems.

Pakistan has recently elected a set of representatives to the national parliament and the four provincial assemblies after three years of military rule. This is the sixth general election in 17 years. The most striking aspect is the strong emergence, on a large scale, of a religious alliance opposed to the US presence in the region. Religious parties had never previously won more than 10 seats or 5 per cent of the total vote in 56 years of Pakistan's existence. The results indicate significant opposition to Musharraf's strong support for the United States as well as his promise to curb Islamic extremism.

MMA - which stands for Muttahida Majlis-e-Amal in Pakistan's state lingo, Urdu - has made a clean sweep of the provincial legislature in the North-West Frontier Province and is likely to govern the south-western Balochistan province. Created after the collapse of the Taliban rule in adjoining Afghanistan, the MMA is opposed to Pakistan's participation in the war on terror and wants the United States to pull out its troops from Pakistan. It identifies with the Taliban and censures Musharraf for apprehending Taliban and Al-Qaeda leaders and handing them over to the American establishment. The emergence of six religious parties under the banner of MMA is seen in political circles as a major setback for the pro-Musharraf PML(QA), dubbed the "King's Party" in the local media.

However, critics of Musharraf assert that he has used his alliance with radical Muslim clerics to provide legitimacy to his dictatorship, facilitating the formation of an influential and destructive "military-mosque" nexus. Islam in Pakistan is highly varied, with multiple versions and modes of faith. With a population of approximately 77 per cent Sunni and 20 per cent Shia, a majority of Pakistanis follow the Hanafi fiqh, or body of laws, and adhere to one of two fundamental schools of interpretation - Deobandi or Barelvi. A third group, the Wahhabi-influenced Ahle Hadith, does not accept the interpretative traditions of the Hanafi school.

Each of these three interpretations of Islam has had its own political face in a given dispensation to pursue domestic and international religio-political agendas. Jamaat-e-Islami (JI) is the most prominent exemplar and forms the nucleus of the present religious alliance, the MMA. Other major radical parties include Jamiat ul Ulema-e-Islam (JUI), a Deobandi organisation, and Jamaat ul Ulema-e-Pakistan (JUP), a Barelvi organisation. JI is closely associated with banned terrorist organisations such as Hizbul Mujahideen and Al-Badr. Jamaat-ud-Dawa (formerly Dawat-ul-Irshad) and its jihadi wing, Lashkar-e-Taiba, are the best-known Ahle Hadith organisations and pursue an international jihadi agenda recognising no frontiers.

In the post-election scenario, there must be no illusions about the "progressive" democratic institutions promised by Musharraf, given the success of these jihadi elements, which have grown in strength as Musharraf's popularity has hit a new nadir because of his pro-US policies. Domestic unrest in Pakistan is also largely attributed to these fundamentalist organisations. Deobandi madrassahs are associated with sectarian violence - Sipah-e-Sahaba Pakistan (SSP) and Lashkar-e-Jhangvi Pakistan (LJP) being the terrorist outfits that fight the three principal Shia militant groups: Sipah-e-Mohammad Pakistan (SMP), Tehrik-e-Jafria Pakistan (TJP) and the Imamia Students Organization. They are also involved in a series of attacks on institutions of the Barelvi faith. As religious organisations assume a dominant role in Pakistan's political spectrum, their agenda of transforming the country into a theocratic state gains momentum, with unrest becoming the order of the day.

The rise of these organisations is largely attributed to the policies followed by successive rulers of Pakistan. General Zia-ul-Haq gave his dictatorial rule legitimacy through Islam. When he came to power in 1977, he chose Deobandi mullahs for patronage, and since then their influence has grown rapidly. By administering an official zakat (religious tithe), he ensured that money was automatically deducted from bank balances and distributed to organisations primarily associated with Deobandi or Ahle Hadith beliefs.

Critics of Musharraf charge him with creating the political space for Islamic religious organisations that now pose a serious challenge to the Pakistani state and to his own leadership. Many believe the General is slowly reaching an "eyeball-to-eyeball" confrontation with the jihadis. Another school of thought argues that Musharraf has skilfully exploited the tendencies toward confrontation and polarisation among Pakistan's political parties for his own ends. The religious parties' astonishing performance may not immediately threaten Musharraf's grip on power, but it could well push him to reconsider the depth of his coalition with Washington's war on terror.

GENERAL Musharraf has repeatedly promised a "deep-rooted" and "sustainable" democratic dispensation, something that does not appear forthcoming, given that the very basis - a constitutional framework - is itself questionable. The Constitution of August 1973 effectively expired in 1985, and what has been in force since then, constitutional experts argue, is a "basic law" crafted without public participation. Z. A. Bhutto managed to have the constitution amended seven times between its promulgation and his removal from office. During the Zia-Junejo era, the Eighth Amendment was passed in 1985, altering as many as 67 articles to impose on the nation a particular and convenient variety of Islam.

In his third year in power, in 2002, Musharraf introduced his own revisions to suit his policies through the Legal Framework Order (LFO), gazetted in August and affecting some 30 articles of the constitution. Supporters of the present military regime argue that this was done to check interruptions in the democratic process caused by institutional failure, citing two reasons: centralisation of power and abdication of responsibility by legislators. Political observers, however, point out that the changes will undermine the parliamentary system. Analysts believe the powerful military junta is entrenching a permanent political role for itself at the expense of the prime minister. The claim that a future parliament will be able to amend the new legislation inspires little confidence; no measure introduced by a military government has been overturned by parliament except on two occasions.

Through these amendments, Musharraf has taken a leaf out of the books of his predecessors - Iskander Mirza, Ayub Khan, Yahya Khan and Zia-ul-Haq - by arming himself with the power to dissolve parliament and dismiss the prime minister should the need arise. He has also checkmated his two principal rivals, Benazir Bhutto and Nawaz Sharif, by barring them from contesting elections. In this endeavour, the judiciary has played an important role by upholding its legislation, once again allowing itself to serve the narrow interests of the military-intelligence establishment, with national interest relegated to the margins.

All these developments have reduced Pakistan to what Western analysts describe as a "diminished client" state, dependent on US diplomatic, economic and military support. The success of Islamic forces, combined with the lack of a genuine basis for democratic governance, spells more trouble for the West. Despite US pressure, Pakistan has shown an unwillingness or inability to curb the illegal political power of these groups. Weak institutions and a poor education system have made the country a source of insecurity and instability in South Asia.

Musharraf - Chief of Army Staff, President and Chief Executive - needs to address his domestic constituency as a priority instead of indulging in anti-India rhetoric like "Kashmir runs in our blood." It is also imperative for him to recognise that the US and Pakistan share neither history nor culture, and that the common thread binding them may fray if pro-Taliban forces consolidate power in the two provinces bordering Afghanistan. In the post-December 13 scenario, Islamabad used the threat of nuclear escalation to press Washington into vetoing possible Indian military action. Next time, if Musharraf cannot rein in his own jihadi forces or again embarks on adventurism, it may spell doom for his own stability as Pakistan's ruler.

3.4 PAKISTAN: LOOKING INTO ITS STATECRAFT

December 2002

George W. Bush has, in recent times, earned the dubious distinction of radicalising Muslims into anti-American postures, setting in motion conditions that have enabled pro-Islamic forces to assume dominant roles in government formation in two Muslim countries - Turkey and Pakistan. The sweeping victory of an Islamist-rooted party in secular Turkey is a vivid case in point. This facilitation has come about because of US one-upmanship in the world order, resulting in a sharp polarisation of countries into Islamic and non-Islamic blocs - a division that had appeared to fade after the break-up of the erstwhile USSR. With Washington now pursuing an agenda widely perceived in the Islamic world as anti-Muslim, the recent setbacks should surprise no one.

The broad electoral victory in Turkey of the Justice and Development Party (AKP), a party with Islamic roots, marks a journey into uncharted waters. That its leader, Recep Tayyip Erdogan, is a practising Muslim who was once active in the Islamist movement merely completes the grim picture for Western capitals. AKP has secured an absolute majority in the Turkish Grand National Assembly, but the one ray of hope for Western establishments lies in Turkey's powerful military elite, which has historically played a pivotal role in checking the rise of Islamist forces - unlike Pakistan, where large sections of the omnipotent military have nurtured them.

The United States has also handed fundamentalist Islamic forces in Pakistan an extraordinary opportunity. Maulana Fazlur Rahman - the MMA's prime-ministerial candidate - could scarcely have imagined that, thanks in part to Uncle Sam, he would become a serious contender for power. The

Muttahida Majlis-e-Amal (MMA), a religious alliance comprising Jamaat-e-Islami (JEI) of Qazi Hussain Ahmad, Jamiat-ul-Ulema-e-Islam (JUI) of Maulana Fazlur Rahman, JUI of Maulana Sami-ul-Haq, Jamiat-ul-Ulema-e-Pakistan (JUP) of Shah Ahmed Noorani, Markazi Jamiat Ahle Hadith (MJAH) of Sajid Mir and Tehrik-e-Islami of Sajid Naqvi, quickly converted anti-American sentiment into votes and emerged as a formidable political force.

The MMA has secured 45 seats - an unprecedented 18 per cent of the National Assembly - in addition to control of one provincial government and a share in a second. This makes it a major political player rather than the marginal force it once was. The strong showing of these religious parties raises serious doubts about how Islamabad will deal with a political bLine of Control hostile to its ties with the United States and inclined to push a hard line toward India. Analysts believe the MMA will do its utmost to loosen government restraints on Islamic militants and to sustain Pakistani support for the Kashmir insurgency. It will press Musharraf to limit the role of US law-enforcement agencies pursuing Taliban and Al-Qaeda fugitives, particularly in districts where the MMA is part of the provincial government. If Washington ignores these signals and, against all wise counsel, pursues war against Iraq, the world order may be irreversibly altered; such a war would surely consolidate anti-American sentiment and could even trigger Musharraf's overthrow by a hard-line Islamist general.

The MMA's victories, some analysts argue, could also furnish Musharraf with a convenient alibi to resist US pressure to dismantle the terrorist infrastructure directed against India. The elections are likely to encourage his efforts to revitalise the old alliance between the army and the religious right, while the MMA will undoubtedly seek to deepen its influence in Kashmir and persuade the military elite to continue jihad there. In the short term, these results pose little threat to Musharraf's dominance of decision-making, but in the longer run the MMA could profoundly affect Pakistan's domestic stability, sectarian violence and the degree of radical penetration inside the armed forces – all of which should alarm him.

Western analysts, however, regard General Pervez Musharraf as merely another in a long line of inept opportunists – military and civilian alike – who have ruled Pakistan over the past half-century. Many predict he will retain power as long as he wishes, barring assassination, but will fail to cleanse the country of its ills. He has kept an ace up his sleeve by decreeing the establishment of a National Security Council (NSC) before the elections, to act as a forum for consultation on strategic matters relating to the sovereignty, integrity and security of the state. This institution is widely seen as central to his and the army's strategy for retaining control over national security, foreign policy and key aspects of domestic politics.

Musharraf took a calculated gamble – not that he had much choice – in kowtowing to the United States after 9/11 on the assumption that the implied monetary benefits would help revive Pakistan's sagging economy. With its finances in shambles, Pakistan seized the chance to ally with Washington in the hope of economic transition, though the depth and systemic nature of its problems make genuine recovery doubtful. Now in its sixth decade of independence, Pakistan still depends heavily on agriculture yet is already forced to import food grains. Water-storage capacity has fallen to roughly one-third of its 1947 level. Over the past 15 years, socio-economic conditions have deteriorated sharply, with poverty soaring from 17 million people in the mid-1980s to nearly 50 million out of a total population of 140 million. A public-policy group estimates that about 38 per cent of Pakistanis live below the poverty line; the World Bank reported in 2000 that 54 per cent of those over 15 – some 46 million people - were illiterate, and its 1999 report recorded an under-five mortality rate of 126 per thousand.

Yet, once Pakistan joined the US-led war on terror, its foreign-exchange reserves began an unprecedented surge. They jumped fivefold from about US$1.5 billion before September 11 to roughly US$7.5 billion, with indications that the upward trend will continue. Analysts attribute this transformation to generous rescheduling of Pakistan's external debt (US$32.5 billion), extended grace periods by creditor countries and a resultant fall in cash outflows for debt servicing. There is widespread speculation that the United States played a key role in securing IMF approval of a long-pending Pakistani request for a generous loan under the Poverty Reduction and Growth Facility, which carries lower interest rates than standard adjustment loans.

To placate domestic opinion, several US allies in the war on terror - Turkey, Saudi Arabia and even Kuwait - have expressed reservations about allowing their bases to be used in a war against Iraq. Such a war would undoubtedly compound Pakistan's domestic troubles and could even lead to the expulsion of US forces from its soil. Islamabad's volte-face on the Taliban has already cost it dearly, rejuvenating Islamist forces and dashing hopes of a transition to the progressive democratic republic ordinary Pakistanis had envisaged. Should the MMA head a future government, it could steer Pakistan toward its own version of an "Islamic revolution", backed by hard-line clerics and radical elements within the army.

America's stated goal in the region, analysts concede, is to eliminate terrorists who threaten US lives and interests and to ensure that Afghanistan remains under an administration responsive to the West and acquiescent to Washington's agenda. Whatever the outcome, however, US interests may be seriously damaged if the MMA ultimately assumes the mantle of governance in Pakistan. Reports from Washington suggest that the US has already moved to broker a deal between Benazir Bhutto's PPP and Musharraf's PML-Q with the singular objective of keeping the MMA out of power. Washington knows exactly how to exploit a state beleaguered by violence, illiteracy, corruption, poverty, religious extremism and tribalism to serve its purposes in South Asia. It has no intention of jeopardising its relationship with Pakistan, which it views as a modestly nuclear-armed, small-time partner willing to carry out low-end military tasks on America's broader strategic agenda.

3.5 PAKISTAN'S NEW PM: OLD WINE, NEW BOTTLE

December 2002

General Pervez Musharraf, President of Pakistan, is a pleased fellow these days; after all, his poster boy, the 58-year-old Mir Zafarullah Khan Jamali, is the chosen one to play second fiddle to him as the new Prime Minister.

Musharraf, hereafter referred to as You Know Who, to borrow a Harry Potterism, has facilitated this turn of fortune by murdering with a borrowed knife; after all, that is what he is good at. Splitting the PPP did not prove to be very knotty, even though in the given scenario, it did prove time-consuming. All is well that ends well, and the eventual outcome pleases You Know Who as much as it does (shrub-grown-to-) Bush, sitting pretty in the US of A. For the MMA, the religious alliance and tactical irritant, the hatchet is officially buried.

A thousand dreams have come crashing down for Rehman, the prime ministerial candidate of the MMA, who was, till yesterday, sitting pretty and at one point was even pronounced the PM of Pakistan (sorry, Mr Dependable, PTI, you jumped the gun). The installation of Jamali in the top post makes You Know Who invincible, and to underestimate him is a gross injustice to his latent talent.

In the first place, You Know Who tried his level best to broker a deal with Benazir Bhutto through their mutual American friends. However, no sooner did the PPP start exploring a possible tie-up with the untouchable MMA than You Know Who put his state machinery into overdrive to bring about a split in the PPP.

If Jamali's initial statements are any benchmark, he is not going to step on You Know Who's toes and will merrily follow his policies, not that he has much choice. External affairs, Kashmir and the security of Pakistan are issues that are beyond his domain, and he will do his best to toe his benefactor's line. Any deviation would not be good for the health and spirits of the new Wazir-e-Azam.

You Know Who kept an ace up his sleeve by establishing the National Security Council (NSC) by decree before the election, to serve as a forum for consultation on strategic matters about the sovereignty, integrity and security of the state. This institution, many believe, is central to his and the army's strategy for keeping control over national security and foreign policy, and over major aspects of domestic politics.

Jamali, an inveterate party-hopper, is known for his placatory sound-bites aimed at pleasing his masters, who keep changing from time to time. Military rule has always been bliss for You Know Who's chosen boy - first General Zia, and now another benefactor in khaki uniform. During Zia's regime, in 1985, he lost the post of Prime Minister to Mohammad Junejo. Jamali knows exactly how to extract his pound of flesh, and his chameleon-like quality is his "magic weapon" - and an effective one too.

Hailing from Balochistan, Jamali has always been a strong figure in the southern part of the province and was elected Chief Minister in 1988, 1990 and once again in 1996. During the tenure of Z. A. Bhutto, he was an ardent admirer, but no sooner was Bhutto toppled than Jamali switched loyalties to General Zia and was later rewarded with a berth as a federal minister in Junejo's cabinet.

He has also identified himself with Nawaz Sharif's PML, but the party has never been his preference; post is. So, it did not come as a big surprise when he jumped onto the bandwagon of You Know Who's PML(QA). Contrary to what we have been led to believe, working under the shadow of a junta regime will in no way prove difficult for Jamali, who has, time and again, shown that he - and he alone - is the right stooge for the coveted post.

He also shares a rare distinction - if one may take the liberty of calling it that - with You Know Who. Neither gentleman do not belong to the all-powerful traditional Punjabi section of the populace, which has, over the years, thrown up most candidates for the top posts in Pakistan. While Musharraf is a Mohajir, the new Prime Minister was born into the Jamali tribe in Balochistan province. But as long as he enjoys the pleasure of the all-powerful army, these trivial things are of no major concern in the given dispensation.

The joke doing the rounds in Islamabad these days concerns the hullabaloo surrounding the Constitution of Pakistan, promulgated first in 1973. While the anti-You Know Who brigade argues that it took oath under the original version of the Constitution, the pro-You Know Who lobby among parliamentarians insists that this was done under the amended version, with the Legal Framework Ordinance, issued by You Know Who just before the elections - an integral part of the scheme of things.

With Jamali taking over the mantle of governance, many believe that You Know Who has acquired a lethal weapon - a front, strictly speaking - to carry out his unpopular decisions, which also gives him an effective alibi for plausible deniability should things deviate from the set course.

The installation of Jamali, in a nutshell, poses little danger to You Know Who's dominance of decision-making, but in the long term, the MMA, the vocal opposition in the National Assembly, could have an important bearing on Pakistan's domestic stability, sectarian violence and radical clout inside the armed forces.

You Know Who is just another in the long line of ham-handed opportunists - military and civilian alike - who have ruled Pakistan over the past five decades. And You Know Who will be able to hold on to power as long as he desires, unless he is eliminated, but he will not be able to clean the country.

For the time being, Jamali is more than perfect to serve him to his satisfaction.

3.6 BANGLADESH: PAKISTAN'S ALTER EGO

December 2002

Ever since Bangladesh came into being in 1971, many of its 130 million people have had an 'identity crisis' of sorts over whether they are Bengalis first or whether their Muslim faith should take primacy in their lives. For centuries, Bengalis have been unified by a culture of tolerance that cuts across the usual South Asian division between Hindu and Muslim. Ironically, a similar crisis has surfaced in Kashmir over time - whether to identify with Kashmiriat, an ethos and way of life, or to let religious identity as Muslims become the dominant parameter shaping their political future.

The portrayal of Bangladesh as a country where fundamentalism is flourishing comes as a rude shock to many of its Muslims, given that the nation was born out of a civil war against religious bigotry. Yet two schools of thought have always coexisted: one that cleaves to the "spirit of 1971", and another that still follows the two-nation theory and relates to the "spirit of 1947". The former's protagonists now sit in opposition, while the latter are a key part of the present regime. It is in this context that the success of fundamentalists in spreading their network must be examined.

Bangladesh is no Afghanistan - or even Pakistan - but after 15 years under martial rule, the democracy restored in 1990 remains fragile. The hostility between the Awami League, voted out at the end of its term in July 2001, and the Bangladesh Nationalist Party, the largest party in the four-party alliance government, has little to do with ideology and is largely driven by personal animosity between their leaders. Jamaat-e-Islami, which once opposed Bangladesh's independence from Pakistan and is now in government, is believed to have nurtured Islamic jihadis and to be the main force behind the astonishing proliferation of unlicensed madrasas over the past decade. Estimates suggest there are 20,000–25,000 such schools (and some 190,000 mosques), many dedicated to propagating ultra-fundamentalist ideology and, in some cases, imparting arms training.

Islami Oikya Jote (IOJ), a right-wing party, is another important member of Begum Khaleda Zia's government. The pro-Pakistan Jamaat-e-Islami holds 16 seats in parliament and controls two powerful ministries under Maulana Matiur Rahman Nizami and Ali Ahsan Mohammad Mujahid. Both Islamist parties have a history of links to terror outfits. IOJ is a known sympathiser and supporter of Islamic fundamentalism, the now-defunct Taliban and Al-Qaeda, and analysts point out that it is closely associated with Harkat-ul-Jehad-ul-Islami (HUJI), an organisation said to have been patronised by Osama bin Laden since 1993.

The presence of two hard-line parties in government suggests that Bangladesh is tempted to shed its traditionally moderate Bengali image, a trend confirmed by repeated attacks on members of the Hindu minority by Islamic hardliners linked to elements within the state. The previous Awami League government had tried to curb these forces, arresting several leaders and cadres, but the new right-wing regime has clearly created a more sympathetic climate for extremist operations. HUJI, headed by Showkat Osman (a.k.a. Sheikh Farid) with Imtiaz Quddus as general secretary, is believed to command around 13,000 cadres and to run six to eight arms-training camps in the Chittagong hill tracts. Its recruits come chiefly from madrasa students and maintain close links with Indian terrorist groups in the Northeast, such as ULFA, while coordinating with Pakistan's ISI, which offers patronage.

Many regard HUJI as an extended arm of Al-Qaeda in Bangladesh. It has carried out multiple attacks inside the country and maintains documented ties with Jaish-e-Mohammed (Jaish-e-Mohammed) and Lashkar-e-Toiba in Pakistan and Bangladesh. HUJI has been implicated in scores of bombings, including two assassination attempts on Prime Minister Sheikh Hasina in July 2000, and finds natural allies among Muslim guerrillas from India sheltering across the border and among Rohingya Muslims who have fled Burmese repression. Analysts note that HUJI receives financial assistance from Pakistan, Saudi Arabia and Afghanistan through Muslim NGOs such as Adarsa Kutir, Al-Faruk Islamic Foundation and Hataddin. It has been at the forefront of recruiting Bangladeshi and Indian Muslims to fight in Jammu and Kashmir under Harkat-ul-Mujahideen, even as Indian insurgent groups in the Northeast continue to enjoy sanctuary and operational bases on Bangladeshi soil.

A significant section of Bangladeshis believes their country cannot insulate itself from the fundamentalist agenda and may be in no better position than Pakistan, given that right-wing elements have secured real power and representation. Tackling them head-on, analysts warn, could provoke a violent backlash. Both Islamist coalition partners increasingly use front organisations and cut-outs to preserve plausible deniability if circumstances demand. In the post-9/11 climate, Jamaat-e-Islami has tried to project a more moderate face and, according to observers, has delegated militant operations to its student wing, Islami Chhatra Shibir, which has been linked to a series of bombings and killings. Publicly, Jamaat-e-Islami pledges support to the war on terror, but beneath the surface, it continues to aid and abet jihad in India and Afghanistan.

Despite its formal commitment against international terrorism, Bangladesh has yet to fully curb covert assistance to groups operating against India. The Directorate-General of Forces Intelligence (DGFI), an arm of the Bangladeshi military, is known to maintain close ties with Pakistan's ISI, which reportedly uses Islamabad's high commission in Dhaka as a hub for its activities. The Americans, meanwhile, prefer a conciliatory approach, largely overlooking allegations that senior Al-Qaeda cadres are hiding in Bangladesh and offering strong backing to the Khaleda Zia government. They are not unaware of the turbulence caused by the rise of right-wing forces, but their policy remains remarkably consistent with their stance on Pakistan: both Dhaka and Islamabad have pledged "strong support" to the US-led war on terror and are treated accordingly.

Khaleda Zia took a leaf out of Musharraf's book when, in the wake of 9/11, she declared that Bangladesh stood solidly with the Bush administration in fighting global terrorism and positioned herself as a staunch member of the international coalition. Despite growing evidence to the contrary, Washington continues to underestimate the long-term threat the country could pose. Ironically, President George W. Bush, in a recent letter to the new Bangladeshi President, Prof. Iajuddin Ahmed, lauded Bangladesh's commitment to combating terrorism - a tribute that sits uneasily with the realities on the ground.

3.7 US: ENGAGING IN DOUBLE-SPEAK

February 2003

This response is not an antagonism of US foreign policy per se, but a pragmatic and judicious examination of why the US is doing what it is doing, particularly in South Asia in general and in the Indian subcontinent in particular. Mr Richard Haass appears to base his assertions on much-used and tired American postulations, with the singular objective of justifying Washington's own flawed policies in the region.

Contrary to what Mr Haass would have us believe, the major stumbling block in India-US relations has been the Bush administration's tendency to conduct its relations with New Delhi through the prism of its relationship with its client state, Pakistan. His claim that the US does not wish to operate through this prism is simply too naïve and ought not to be taken seriously, especially when one looks at ground realities, which suggest otherwise. Washington's obsession with finishing off the remnants of Al Qaeda in its so-called "war against terror" makes Pakistan important to its objectives; consequently, the US chooses to overlook the fact that its staunch ally is itself an epicentre of terrorist infrastructure in the region.

Let us not forget that this fight is as much in Pakistan as it is in Afghanistan. Nor should we be under any illusion about the MMA, the religious coalition that is in power or sharing power in towns along the Afghan border: its leaders are staunch supporters of Osama bin Laden, and it is only natural for them to provide refuge to Al Qaeda fugitives fleeing Afghanistan. Cooperation from Pakistan is therefore expected, but whether it is actually forthcoming is debatable. Powerful sections within Pakistan - including parts of the ISI and the army - continue to sympathise with the Taliban and Al Qaeda, which means the fight is far from over.

Mr Haass's assertion that relations between India and Pakistan are less developed than those between the US and the USSR at the height of the Cold War is too simplistic and naïve to merit serious comment, even as he follows the standard American practice of painting a lurid picture of "dangerous times" with "no or little lines of communication" between the neighbours. He is, however, quite right that everyone should act to ensure the continued sanctity of the Line of Control. But sanctity cannot be reduced to unilateral re-mapping alone; it must also mean an end to infiltration and, consequently, cross-border terrorism. He should not use the term "sanctity" so conveniently or loosely.

Pakistan has not ended its policy of state-sponsored terrorism, and to expect that it will end cross-border terrorism is simply not prudent. This remains true despite the US "urging" General Musharraf, time and again, to do so. He continues to look the other way because he is in a position to do so. To say that the onus of responsibility for resolving bilateral issues lies more with General Musharraf than with Prime Minister Vajpayee is merely to state the obvious. Nevertheless, Washington continues to preach "magnanimity" and "generosity" to India, virtues we are expected to display towards Islamabad. Is this a prudent argument?

The claim that the United States stands "shoulder to shoulder" with India in our battle against terrorism is, to borrow a phrase from Yasser Arafat, a "big, big lie." The US has quite clearly applied double standards in its fight against terrorism, drawing a sharp distinction between its own war on terror and our struggle against cross-border terrorism aided and abetted by Pakistan. Instead of taking India's contentions seriously, it has persisted in justifying the wrongs of its client state. We might have credited Mr Haass's assertion that US policy has been consistent had Washington acted against Pakistan in the larger interests of world peace.

Instead, the US has further strengthened the junta regime

of a Pakistani dictator by lavishing discretionary assistance upon him. A more realistic course would have been to isolate Islamabad through economic sanctions. But nothing of the sort was attempted, because Pakistan is seen as central to American interests in the region and, as in the past, the US will ignore the obvious - and pay dearly for it at some later stage.

We are also at a loss to understand what Mr Haass describes as "positive trends" in Pakistan. These cannot possibly include the rise of the MMA, a pro-Taliban religious party, in such a big way. Nor can they include the installation of Musharraf's poster-boy Jamali as Prime Minister after elections that were, even by European Union standards, a mockery of democratic norms. Still less can the clandestine transfer of nuclear know-how by Islamabad to Pyongyang, in breach of every non-proliferation norm, be described as a "positive trend." Who is hoodwinking whom, and to what purpose, is an open and debatable question.

In the post-13/12 situation, amid heightened tensions between the two neighbours, the Western media went into overdrive to paint a picture of nuclear holocaust should India launch pre-emptive strikes against terrorist infrastructure across the Line of Control. This was done, Mr Haass will forgive the observation, with the singular objective of putting India on the back foot. Coupled with travel advisories issued by Western countries and other "friendly" allies, the campaign had a direct bearing on the prospects of even a limited war, let alone, a full-scale conflict, between the two states.

Such a campaign, unleashed by Western governments with the tacit support of their media fraternities, emboldened Pakistan to stoop so low as to engage in nuclear blackmail against New Delhi. And that pattern, regrettably, continues to this day.

CHAPTER 4: GOVERNANCE, FAULTLINES AND CREDIBILITY

If Chapters 2 and 3 explain the gunman and the state that sends him. Chapter 4 turns back to Srinagar and New Delhi to ask an uncomfortable question: what did we do with the political space that ordinary Kashmiris created in 2002-2003? In this section, I focus on governance, regional fault lines and the erosion of credibility that flowed not from Pakistan's actions but from our own choices. My argument is that even as voters braved bullets to endorse constitutional politics, successive governments in Jammu and Kashmir and at the Centre failed to build institutions and policies worthy of that courage, and in doing so left room for both separatists and jihadists to claim the moral high ground.

I begin with the PDP-Congress coalition that emerged from the 2002 elections. On paper, it represented a fresh start after years of National Conference dominance; in practice, it was hobbled by clashing instincts. The PDP leadership spoke of "healing touch", hinted at dialogue with separatists and projected itself as a softer, Valley-centric alternative; Congress, anchored in national politics, could not openly endorse any dilution of India's sovereign claim or security posture. In my essays, I show how this coalition tried to ride two horses at once—promising firmness to Delhi and empathy to separatists—and ended up sending contradictory signals to both. Confidence-building steps that might have been defensible as part of a wider integration strategy instead appeared as stand-alone concessions in a vacuum of strategic clarity.

From there, I dig into the deeper structural fault lines inside Jammu and Kashmir, particularly the persistent sense of marginalisation in Jammu and Ladakh. The Valley's political class spoke of "Kashmir" as if it were synonymous with the entire state, while large sections of the population in Jammu and Ladakh experienced the special status and Valley-centric governance as a double burden: neither fully part of the national mainstream, nor fairly represented in the state's own power structures. I argue that any durable solution had to address this imbalance—through fairer delimitation, equitable development, and recognition that the state was not a monolith but a mosaic of distinct regions and identities. Instead, for much of the 2002–2003 period, the coalition's energy was consumed by managing day-to-day crises and placating Valley-based players.

Another core strand of this chapter is the crisis of credibility in governance. I examine how corruption, patronage-based administration and the politicisation of security decisions eroded public trust. When governments release hardened militants under the banner of reconciliation but fail to deliver basic governance in refugee camps or ensure justice for victims, people draw their own conclusions. I highlight how Kashmiri Pandit refugees continued to languish in inadequate camps, how displaced communities felt invisible in the grand narratives, and how slogans about "return with dignity" were not matched by concrete rehabilitation plans. In my view, this gap between rhetoric and reality on governance undermined the Indian state's legitimacy in ways that Pakistan could never have managed alone.

The most personal part of this chapter comes when I reflect on the generation of Kashmiri leaders who came of age around me—Mirwaiz Umar Farooq, Omar Abdullah, Sajjad Lone and others. Eventually, we shared a fractured political landscape. In these essays, I illustrate how personal histories, family legacies and competing ambitions are mapped onto larger ideological divides: separatism dressed in religious authority, dynastic nationalism tied to Delhi, and smaller formations trying to carve out space in between. The point I make is that leadership in Kashmir was as much about competing myths and mandates as about policies, and that Delhi consistently misread these personal dynamics.

Chapter 4, taken as a whole, makes three claims. First, that without credible, clean and regionally balanced governance, even a fair election like that of 2002 cannot by itself stabilise a conflict-ridden state. Second, that ignoring the grievances of Jammu, Ladakh and displaced communities while speaking only in the name of the Valley created a legitimacy deficit that separatists exploited. Third, that India's political class—both in Srinagar and Delhi—too often managed, rather than resolved, these contradictions, hoping that time itself would do the heavy lifting.

Seen from today, after delimitation exercises, the assertion of Union Territory control, and a more explicit recognition of Jammu and Ladakh as stakeholders in their own right, this chapter reads as both diagnosis and warning. The failures I describe here help explain why incremental reforms under a special-status regime could never produce the stability that full constitutional integration and a firmer security doctrine have begun to achieve. If Chapters 2 and 3 establish why external drivers of terror had to be confronted, Chapter 4 reminds us that internal governance failures also had to be corrected for Jammu and Kashmir to move from perpetual crisis to a more durable normalcy.

4.1 WILL THIS HOUSEBOAT FLOAT OR SINK?

November 2002

The palaver that unfolded in the post-election milieu in Kashmir has come to a close. The unfolding drama proved to be a pure adrenaline-and-testosterone level of high political adventure. The music has stopped, and the game of musical chairs has ended with the Congress chief, Sonia Gandhi, lackadaisically - much against the wishes of her party colleagues and New Delhi (read BJP) - conceding the post of chief minister to Mufti Mohammad Sayeed, the chief of the People's Democratic Party (PDP). In the process, she has extracted her pound of flesh by not only dictating the provisos of the common minimum programme (CMP), but also ensuring that the mantle of the coordination committee (CC) will be in the hands of Ghulam not-so-Azad, whose position would be akin to that of George Fernandes (you have company) in the National Democratic Alliance at the Centre. Congress is also likely to assume the important post of speaker in the legislative assembly.

Madam has killed two birds with one stone. First, by yielding the CM's position to the PDP, she has displayed magnanimity and generosity - a phenomenon not so often in practice - which will undoubtedly earn her some points as a leader en route to political maturity (sorry, M. J. Akbar, can't take away the credit). Second, she has effectively ensured that the radical programme the PDP wanted to implement is toned down to suit the interests of the Indian National Congress. Of the 31-point CMP mutually agreed upon, 17 points are devoted to the restoration of peace and normalcy and to curbing corruption. The issue of devolution of more powers to the state, however, finds no visible mention in the document.

In doing so, the Congress chief has upset the rank and file of her party in the Jammu region, but things are not entirely gloomy; Jammu will have a deputy chief minister, though the local leadership still feels that, given the numerical advantage Congress had over the PDP, the CM's post should have been theirs. For now, at least, nobody is going to complain and invite the wrath of Madam. The way the father–daughter duo of the Mufti clan has conducted themselves in regionalising the issue of chief ministership has left people in Jammu feeling aggrieved at the step-motherly treatment meted out to them. A large section of Congressmen in the state fear that Mr Sayeed may recommend dissolution of the assembly after completing his three-year tenure, robbing Congress of any chance to head the government.

The maverick chief of the Panthers Party (PP), Prof. Bhim Singh, is a known renegade who, after vehemently opposing Sayeed's candidature, later fell in line at the behest of the Congress chief. Incidentally, this is the same gentleman who initially opposed the entire election process on the premise (or was it the excuse) that voter lists were not updated, and even petitioned the Supreme Court – it would seem at the behest of certain separatist elements (read People's Conference).

The poster boy of the National Conference (NC), Omar Abdullah, is not, as we have been led to believe, going to spend time reading Robert Ludlum (recommended read: Bourne trilogy). He and his golfer dad will be waiting for the right opportunity to topple the Congress–PDP government, particularly given that Farooq Abdullah and Congress have hardly been best of friends. After the June 1983 elections, Congress(I) pursued a policy of total confrontation with the NC government; Mrs G dismissed Farooq Abdullah's ministry on July 2, 1984, and, with Congress(I) support, G. M. Shah (Farooq's estranged brother-in-law) took over as chief minister.

A reconciliation of sorts followed in 1986 with the Rajiv-Farooq accord, but that too was short-lived, and Farooq found himself retreating to the safe havens of London with the advent of V. P. Singh at the helm in New Delhi. The hurt of having been dismissed by Mrs G still rankles Abdullah senior, and to assume that he would not, in due course, seek to oust the coalition government would be to ignore the obvious. The NC think-tank also believes the present arrangement is more a government of compulsion than one rooted in convictions. Farooq's cultivated disdain for Congress, combined with his refusal to continue as caretaker CM even at Atal Bihari Vajpayee's request, epitomises his care-a-damn attitude.

The BJP, his recent partner in politics (read honeymoon), also has much at stake with elections in nine states not far off and the Gujarat polls around the corner. Contrary to public postures, the BJP is likely to make things difficult for Srinagar. Much will eventually depend on whether the PMO – where Sayeed's pilot (read A. S. Dulat, former RAW chief) is on deputation and still working on Kashmir – extends an olive branch to the PDP, or whether the Home Ministry under L. K. Advani prevails. In the event, Advani's response to Srinagar is likely to be a stiff upper lip. This is the bottom line; take it or leave it.

"Daddy's good girl", Mehbooba Mufti has, without doubt, grown by leaps and bounds and will play a crucial role in the process, but it remains to be seen whether the vigour with which she has propelled herself to her present position will translate into a process where the genuine aspirations of the people she speaks for are actually met. For now, we are witnessing placatory sound-bites which, unless translated into practice, remain hollow and meaningless.

The "third front" of the coalition government, whose agenda is in some respects more extreme than the PDP's, will not want to be left behind and will assert itself to ensure its presence is felt. Many believe this constituent will prove the chief tactical irritant. Watch out for Ghulam Sofi, the proxy candidate of the People's Conference, who is certain to play a key role in negotiations with the separatists of the Hurriyat Conference; his cloak-and-dagger relationship with them is common knowledge. In arriving at a "broad-based consensus", the political will of the combine will be tested to the hilt when it opens direct channels of communication with the Hurriyat Conference and other segments of public opinion.

The PDP chief will assume office under very difficult circumstances; what he inherits from Farooq Abdullah is a grim legacy of misrule and militancy. One can only hope he will take all his coalition partners into confidence, avoid any "family squabbles" within the alliance and do his best under the circumstances. Hopes are many and stakes are high - and the world is watching.

4.2 MUFTI: BETWEEN THE DEVIL AND THE DEEP SEA

December 2002

"I wrote my novel, Mr Stone And The Knight's Companion, in Kashmir. I'd like to re-visit it." - Nobel laureate Sir V. S. Naipaul

The other segments of public opinion in Kashmir have adopted an antagonistic approach to the PDP-led coalition government headed by Mufti Sayeed, which severely hampers the ruling coalition's efforts to arrive at a "broad-based consensus." If the statements of JKLF chief Yasin Malik and former Hurriyat Conference chairman Mirwaiz Omar Farooq are any indication, the separatists are not only sticking to their guns but also using every opportunity to take potshots at the PDP.

This makes Sayeed's assignment all the more difficult. Time and again - despite the lack of enthusiasm from New Delhi - he has shown a resolute determination to give his "holistic approach" an honest try. His contention that he must set his own house in order first, before attempting to undo the dreadlocks of the larger Kashmir issue, has, despite separatist reservations, found favour with many ordinary Kashmiris as well as a section of the Indian media.

For years, Srinagar's point of view rarely appeared on the national media horizon. Of late, however, the media does not blindly follow leads and hints from the Home Ministry, but often takes a more balanced view - something that has gone down well in the Valley. The diabolical attack on the historic and symbolic Raghunath temple recently did, however, prompt some mainstream papers to swing over to the Home Ministry's hard-line, questioning Sayeed's supposedly soft approach to militancy. One leading daily, despite a strong

Srinagar bureau, jumped on the hawkish bandwagon when it front-paged reactions to the Raghunath temple outrage.

Even so, Sayeed cannot, and should not, be squarely blamed for that despicable act. It should not be forgotten that when the same shrine was attacked in March, the BJP's coalition partner, the National Conference, was in power. During Farooq Abdullah's tenure innumerable similar attacks occurred, coupled with large-scale killings of minorities, especially in the Jammu region - a record that shows Abdullah senior in a very poor light.

Sayeed's fundamental problem is rooted not so much in his coalition partners as in the separatist elements who, until yesterday, quietly patronised him and offered clandestine support with the singular objective of sending Abdullah packing. Having reassessed the situation, they now appear to believe they have no option but to attack Sayeed - something they consider essential for their own survival as a political force.

It is in this context that one should read the rhetoric of Yasin Malik, the terrorist-turned-politician who now spends much of his time addressing public gatherings in the state, using the platform to lambast Sayeed and endlessly raise the "larger" Kashmir issue - precisely what Sayeed wishes, for the moment, to keep under wraps. Malik and those who think like him consider it vital to attack any dispensation, Sayeed or otherwise, so that the separatist bandwagon does not become irrelevant. They are increasingly worried that Sayeed's healing touch might gain traction; if the therapy works, large sections in Kashmir may become indifferent to the Hurriyat Conference and company.

Sayeed is wisely keeping contentious issues on the back burner, and has taken a principled stand that the nuts and bolts of governance must first be put in order before he turns to what other constituencies demand. Hurriyat Conference and company, however, will have none of it; they insist that he address the "larger issue" first, which they see as the root cause of all evil. In their view, Sayeed is making the grave mistake of treating symptoms rather than the disease.

Mirwaiz Omar Farooq recently articulated the Hurriyat Conference line in a television interview, sticking doggedly to the old rhetoric and displaying little flexibility - an approach unlikely to help matters. Despite his reputation as a moderate, his tone throughout was so combative that any early headway on the wider Kashmir question seems unrealistic.

Still, it is to the credit of the Jammu and Kashmir chief minister that, despite repeated provocations, he refuses to trade barbs with the separatists. At the same time, he has avoided positions that would rupture the working relationships the PDP has built over time - in no small measure due to his energetic daughter, Mehbooba Mufti. Yet the PDP chief is adamant on doing things his way, convinced that in the present circumstances, the most effective cure may not be drastic surgery.

Sayeed, to borrow a phrase, is caught between a rock and a hard place - or perhaps between the devil and the deep sea; take your pick. Signals from Kashmir suggest that the widening gap between the stance of the PDP-led combine on the one hand and that of the Hurriyat Conference and its allies on the other may create unforeseen problems for the government. The winter chill, coupled with icy rhetoric, could make the climate far too inclement for anyone's taste. Sir Naipaul, meanwhile, might do well to realise his cherished desire to revisit Kashmir in spring - or better still, in summer. Let, the winter pass.

4.3 JAMMU: DENIAL, DELAY AND DERELICTION

December 2002

Jammu, the winter capital of Jammu & Kashmir, has always had a lame-duck status in the political dispensation and, time and again, has been made to play second fiddle to state administrations headed by Valley-based leaders. Of late, a thousand dreams came crashing down for the people of the Jammu region when the candidature of Ghulam Nabi Azad, who belongs to Doda in Jammu, for the top post was withdrawn in favour of the Valley-based PDP chief, Mufti Sayeed.

The widely reported "denunciation" of statehood for Jammu, inferred from the defeat of BJP and Jammu State Morcha candidates, is a classic example of how the media presents the Jammu and Kashmir predicament to the Indian public. This fits a familiar pattern employed by powers-that-be worldwide in such situations: circumvent certain facts, obfuscate others, then manufacture "facts" that sustain a narrow system of ideas and beliefs. It is imperative to put matters in proper perspective.

First, the BJP's defeat in no way amounts to a rejection of demands for a separate state or, more realistically, for devolution of powers to Jammu through an autonomous regional council – the long-standing demand of a sizeable section of the populace. Denial and delay have pushed some into an aggressive posture, demanding full statehood. Second, these demands are not communal, contrary to what we have been led to believe. Had that been the case, people in Jammu, cutting across party lines and religious denominations, would not have rallied behind a Muslim candidate – Ghulam Nabi Azad – for chief minister. The coalescing of Jammu's secular character is one of the most notable outcomes of the election; it is this strength that, for the first time, allowed the region credibly to stake its claim to the top post.

For as long as anyone can remember, it has been the state of Jammu and Kashmir - three distinct geographical and ethnic regions: Jammu, Kashmir and Ladakh. Jammu is an essential component and has, over the past decade and a half of turmoil, played a crucial role in deterring the overt and covert manoeuvres of Valley separatists. The people of this historic city have stood tall despite all odds, giving a befitting reply to secessionist elements bent on destroying the state's secular fabric.

Given the distribution of populations across the state and the impact of sustained propaganda from across the border, carving out a separate state from within Jammu and Kashmir may not be prudent; the demand carries dangerous implications. Only secularism and a strengthened federal set-up can truly guarantee Jammu's unity and rightful share of political power. A secular, responsive Jammu is, in the long run, also in the Valley's best interests.

The key to protecting Jammu from gradual marginalisation is to keep it on an even political keel. For decades, there has been talk of regional autonomy for the state's various ethnic groupings, and Jammu's claim has been voiced most insistently. Veteran activist Balraj Puri, along with Hari Om, has been the principal champion of this perspective, writing extensively in its favour. Large sections of people in Jammu, Ladakh and among Kashmiri Pandits have openly endorsed this stand. In the larger interest of the state, the Jammu and Kashmir regions must devise a mechanism to function as equal partners.

A sober examination shows that Kashmir enjoys the lion's share of political and administrative clout. Central grants to the state have not been evenly distributed, leaving Jammu and Ladakh without the means to keep pace with the Valley.

Kashmir, with a land area of 15,853 sq. km and less than half the state's population, sends 46 legislators to the 87-member assembly; Jammu, by contrast, covers 26,293 sq. km, has a roughly comparable population, yet returns only 37 MLAs. This political disparity is another major source of resentment.

Between 1966 and 1981, the state government set up three commissions with much fanfare to pacify Jammu: the Gajendragadkar Commission (1967), the Kadri Commission (1972) and the Sikri Commission (1979). The first two were tasked with examining Jammu's grievances and recommending remedies for regional imbalance; the Sikri panel was asked to consider creating additional districts in the region. Successive regimes failed to implement their recommendations, consigning them to the historical dustbin.

On May 9, 1995, the Ladakh Autonomous Hill Development Council Act was enacted, and the Leh Hill Council followed in September 1995. There is no compelling reason why a similar arrangement cannot be fashioned for Jammu. An autonomous council would greatly facilitate economic, cultural, social and political development in a fair, transparent and equitable manner across all three regions. Only such an approach can ensure equal opportunities for development and participation in the state's political affairs. Balraj Puri has rightly stressed the need to reinforce the federal constitutional fabric through decentralisation via a five-tier structure - state, regional, district, block and panchayat.

The great merit of this argument is that, in circumstances increasingly laced with communal tensions, regional identities can offer an alternative rallying point. Regional autonomy thus appears a viable response to the genuine aspirations of Jammu and Ladakh, while also offering, more broadly, a way to ease the Valley's estrangement from the Indian mainstream.

4.4 KASHMIR DIARY: TRUTH, LOVE AND MALICE

October 2002

Kashmir has been aptly described as a "quarter-per-cent conflict" - accounting for roughly one-quarter of one per cent of the combined territory, economy and population of India and Pakistan - and yet it looms disproportionately large in our minds. Day after day, we track events, apply our mathematical instincts and try to "sum up" what is happening, only to feel dragged into a whirlpool with a black hole at its centre, darkness closing in from all sides and no light at the end of the tunnel. The problem has all the makings of an extraordinarily complex yarn of events, stretching beyond our wildest imaginings.

The optimists are having a field day in Kashmir, convinced that the Valley is limping back to normal after a decade of militancy and unrest. An overwhelming response to the electoral process, they argue, will remove miseries and enable elected representatives to address genuine grievances. This school of thought consists of able and competent men who merrily sing to the tune of the state's functionaries: everything is rosy; there is no need to worry; "we will deal with the hawk's hand-in-glove with Musharraf once we are, Inshallah, voted back to power with a thumping majority."

Had circumstances been normal rather than exceptional, one would not have been surprised to see the Abdullah regime thrown out - anti-incumbency is, after all, widely regarded as a useful instrument for sacking unpopular governments. Alas, that realism still seems a distant daydream; the lack of a genuine pluralistic dimension in Kashmir's political spectrum says it all. A divided opposition was the last thing one might have wished for. The BJP has been hand-in-glove with the ruling National Conference; Congress has only just woken from its slumber; and the local entrant, the People's Democratic Party, has been unable to shake off its negative image thanks to its founder-president, Mufti Sayeed. Together, they make up only half the opposition, the other half being the separatists, themselves further divided.

The All Parties Hurriyat Conference and company have finally come to terms with reality, but only after voting themselves out of reckoning by adopting an unyielding stance. By staying away from the polls, they have condemned themselves to another five years of political seclusion, each passing day taking them further from the people they claim to represent. One might go a step further: had the Hurriyat Conference and allies taken part in the elections and emerged as the largest bloc in the assembly, they could have held New Delhi to ransom and, if their genuine demands were denied, resigned en masse, creating a spectacle that would have left both New Delhi and Uncle Sam thoroughly flabbergasted. Instead, they chose to remain "too many cooks", determined to spoil the broth.

At the helm in the Valley today are three young men - Mirwaiz Omar Farooq, Omar Abdullah and Sajjad Lone - with whom the writer shares a distinction (if it may be called that): all attended the same school in Kashmir and learnt the essential lessons of life from the same set of able teachers. Yet, by a quirk of destiny, they now stand poles apart and are more or less at loggerheads.

Over time, there has been a remarkable shift in the mindset of the Valley's majority community - a change to be welcomed. They abhor the gun culture; many now admit, at least in private, that taking up the gun was a grave mistake. There is little use in raking up the past, but the reflection itself is significant. Abdullah junior, after all these years, comes across as an essentially honest and upright man against whom nothing personal should be held. Yet it is impossible to overlook the fact that his esteemed father heads an unpopular establishment that deserves to be voted out for its lax governance and failure to alleviate common suffering. Omar has been seen competently taking on the likes of Barkha Dutt on television; whether he enjoys genuine popularity among his own people is a more fundamental question that only time can answer.

His arch rival, the Mirwaiz, is also a man of considerable talent; on a sunny day one can imagine the two Omars sitting down to share a cup of kahwa. Yet, in true Bollywood fashion, their families are jaani dushman - the Sher (Abdullahs) versus Bakra (Mirwaiz camp) feud is common knowledge. It is both surprising and heartening that the Mirwaiz is still alive and did not fall to the same assassins' bullets that claimed Prof. Lone; both men, after all, shared a vision of restoring peace to the strife-torn Valley and bringing all stakeholders to the negotiating table.

If instincts are right, Mirwaiz Omar Farooq will play an instrumental role in the coming years in ending the ugly reign of the gun and ensuring peace and prosperity. Along with Sajjad Lone and Bilal Lone, he is among the few Hurriyat Conference leaders with genuine mass bases across the Valley and could help fill the political void if the Abdullahs are finally voted out. Whether Sajjad fielded dummy candidates or not remains unclear, but his People's Conference will almost certainly be a significant player in the political arena. With his father's untimely death, Sajjad has stepped into his shoes and taken on the mantle of working for peace and tranquillity, a step that deserves broad support.

In their respective roles as torch-bearers of peace, the trio will, one hopes, do everything in their power to rid the Valley of the menace of terrorism, which by even moderate estimates has claimed far too many lives. Best wishes are extended to all three alumni of the same alma mater, in the hope that they will help eradicate the gun culture that Kashmiris have come to loathe, restore the Valley to its past glory and, last but not least, re-establish Kashmiriat - that cherished way of life so close to our hearts - in letter and spirit.

4.5 JAMMU AND KASHMIR: THE INSIDE STORY

February 2003

The present dispensation headed by Mufti Sayeed in Jammu and Kashmir is moving ahead with positive strides; nevertheless, along the way, a few developments by design or naively may have serious ramifications for its ability to translate electoral promises into concrete achievements. The main opposition party, the National Conference, is monitoring the situation on a day-to-day basis and, though it has stopped short of outright criticism, several recent trends will make its leadership smile for all the right reasons.

The much-awaited expansion of the council of ministers has become a major source of "on the warpath" feelings against the regime, with people in Jammu, the Kashmiri Pandit community and Sikhs all feeling short-changed. The exclusion of Raman Bhalla, a prominent Congress leader from Jammu, has triggered widespread protests in the region, with some of his supporters even attempting self-immolation. Another prominent Dalit woman from Jammu has also been denied a berth, a decision severely criticised by the local press. Despite repeated promises by the Congress leadership on women's representation, the present government does not include even a single token woman minister.

As a result, Congress, if indications are correct, is fast losing ground in Jammu, the very region that sent the largest number of its legislators to the assembly. Congress's loss is the BJP's gain. While the BJP has officially opposed separate statehood for Jammu, the election of Prof. Nirmal Singh as state president means there is every likelihood that pro-statehood forces - RSS, Jammu State Morcha and ABVP - will coalesce around it; Singh is an old RSS man and a former state president of ABVP. The BJP may not perform a formal U-turn on its stated "no trifurcation" line, but that will not stop it from knitting together pro-Hindutva forces into a cohesive bloc, putting real pressure on Congress in the region, especially as the local leadership feels betrayed by the non-inclusion of popular figures in the expanded ministry.

The Sikh minority is also up in arms over its lack of representation. Although the PDP-led government has nominated prominent Jammu farmer leader Trilok Singh Bajwa to the Rajya Sabha, Sikh groups continue to insist that the community has been denied its due at the state level. Some organisations have gone so far as to accuse the state and central governments of staging Sikh massacres with the help of Indian intelligence agencies and have demanded a judicial probe by a sitting Supreme Court judge. Many observers see this hard line as pressure tactics intended to arm-twist the coalition into offering a ministerial berth.

Much praise has been showered on the Sayeed government in the national press for its decision to set up a regional autonomous council for Ladakh (read Leh). Yet noted writer and columnist Balraj Puri told Kashmir Telegraph that the basic premise for such a council should be regional, not religious, concerns. In his view, the mechanism the government has devised rests on religion, thereby defeating the very purpose of a regional development council. Puri warns that this approach risks widening the schism between Muslims (predominantly Shia) and Buddhists - the two principal communities in Ladakh - while the continued delay in establishing a similar body for Jammu sits badly with people there. Congress had promised such an autonomous council in its manifesto, a pledge that contributed greatly to its strong showing; once in coalition with the PDP, however, the party buried the issue. Regional autonomy for Jammu finds no mention in the Common Minimum Programme and is clearly off the current agenda.

Kashmiri Pandits, though a political non-entity, remain vociferous, and their views carry weight. Mufti Sayeed has given the community representation by inducting Raman Mattoo as a minister of state, but this has not pleased many Pandits, who complain that several prominent PDP Pandit leaders have been overlooked. A senior PDP figure told Kashmir Telegraph, on condition of anonymity, that there is considerable resentment in party ranks and within the community at the non-inclusion of veteran leader B. K. Vaishnavi. He noted that Mattoo's constituency recorded a voter turnout of just 1.62 per cent - the lowest in the state - suggesting he lacks a solid base even among his own people.

Vaishnavi has long been a close associate of Mufti Sayeed and has stood by him through thick and thin, so party cadres naturally feel aggrieved. Incidentally, Vaishnavi is also believed to be close to former RAW chief A. S. Dulat, now in the Prime Minister's Office, and there are indications that Dulat is unhappy with Sayeed's decision to leave him out of the ministry.

The trends now emerging may not yet ring alarm bells for the Mufti government, but it is essential that, in his drive to revive the state's economy, he does not - by design or oversight - ignore these warning signals generated by his own policy choices. It is never too late to mend or correct course. One can only hope he will review the situation in retrospect and do whatever he deems necessary to ensure that all three regions, and all sections of society, feel included and in tune with his "healing touch" policy. A tall order, certainly, but not an unachievable one.

4.6 MUFTI SAYEED: THE REAL TEST IS AHEAD

October 2003

One thing continues to puzzle most observers who track developments in Kashmir: how Mufti Sayeed has managed, so far, to accomplish the near-impossible in dealing with Deputy Prime Minister L. K. Advani. Take the release of pro-Pakistan separatist leader Syed Ali Shah Geelani. New Delhi had made it abundantly clear that no mercy would be shown to a man who once described militancy in Kashmir as a "holy war". No doubt his failing health eventually provided the formal basis for parole, but it still took considerable persuasion from Mufti Sayeed to bring Advani round to giving the green signal.

If the first hundred days of Sayeed's government are any indication, the chief minister has enjoyed an unusually smooth run, with his views prevailing on most key policy questions. Whether it was the move to scrap POTA or the contentious decision to disband the Special Operations Group, he has faced little resistance from any quarter, including the main opposition, the National Conference. For the moment, his path has also been eased by the relative lull in militancy (barring the Raghunath temple attack), which has spared him awkward confrontations with New Delhi. Much of this respite, however, owes more to winter than to policy; infiltration traditionally drops sharply in the cold months, constraining militant operations.

Come spring, infiltration will spike again, almost certainly leading to a rise in bloodshed. Melting snows reopen safe havens on the higher ridges of the Pir Panjal, which are largely inaccessible in winter. That is when the PDP-Congress combine will be tested to the hilt. A single major incident could snowball into a national issue - especially with elections to more than half a dozen states on the horizon. Any upsurge in violence in Jammu and Kashmir would instantly be folded into the BJP's revived nationalism narrative, pushed indirectly through the wider Sangh Parivar. In such a climate, whatever conciliatory signals New Delhi has sent the new regime could harden overnight, making life significantly more difficult for Mufti and his colleagues and depriving them of crucial central support.

Signals from the corridors of power in Delhi already suggest that a large section of the BJP opposes any dialogue with separatists at this stage, fearing that engagement would blunt a valuable tactical weapon against Congress in key state contests. The party is leaving no stone unturned to corner its main rival and, if the need arises, will surely accuse Congress of adopting a soft line on militancy in Jammu and Kashmir. One influential faction would prefer to deploy the "Kashmir card" only as a last resort if anti-incumbency, governance failures and local issues fail to deliver the desired electoral impact. Mufti, acutely aware of this dangerous backdrop, has repeatedly urged that Kashmir not be turned into an election plank. Even so, reliable sources suggest he has made little headway with Advani on his proposal for parallel talks with separatist formations and elected legislators; with the BJP's stakes high in the coming assembly polls, the deputy prime minister appears to be having second thoughts.

The forthcoming session of the Jammu and Kashmir assembly will therefore be instructive. Much will depend on how the National Conference chooses to position itself vis-à-vis the ruling coalition. If it launches an all-out assault on the PDP-Congress government over its perceived conciliatory gestures towards "secessionist" elements - fuelled by talk of tacit understandings between Mufti and certain separatist groups - the pitch will be perfectly prepared for the BJP to take up the theme nationally and deploy it against Congress in the campaign trail. Given the party's recent success in

Gujarat on the back of Pakistan-bashing and hard-line rhetoric on terrorism, it is more than likely that Mufti will come under sustained fire for decisions that have not gone down well with the RSS and, in particular, the VHP.

Should militant violence escalate in the coming months - a more than plausible scenario - an element of antagonism could easily creep into relations between the PDP–Congress government in Srinagar and the BJP-led government in New Delhi. The National Conference, as a member of the NDA despite its chequered history with the BJP, is well placed to help corner Congress. Farooq Abdullah's well-known antipathy towards the party may, in fact, spur the NC to mount a scathing attack on the coalition during the assembly session, providing the BJP with ready fodder if it decides to foreground the Kashmir issue in the state polls.

Sayeed Sahib, when winter is here, spring is never far behind - and it is a safe wager that this spring will not be a particularly pleasant one.

CHAPTER 5: KASHMIRIYAT, EXODUS AND THE HUMAN COST

In the earlier chapters, I focus on elections, terror networks and Pakistan's strategic calculus. In Chapter 5, I turn to what all of that meant for people, culture and civilisational memory. This section argues that the conflict in Jammu and Kashmir is not only about borders, sovereignty and security; it is also about the slow strangulation of a plural ethos once described as "Kashmiriyat", and about the near-erasure of a community–the Kashmiri Pandits–that had lived in the Valley for millennia.

I revisit the targeted killings, threats and systematic intimidation that forced the mass exodus of Kashmiri Pandits in the late 1980s and early 1990s, and I examine how little serious political attention this catastrophe received in the decade that followed. Drawing on official figures and human-rights documentation, I highlight the scale of the tragedy: thousands of lives lost directly or indirectly, entire neighbourhoods emptied, over a hundred temples desecrated or destroyed, and tens of thousands of families reduced to living for years in cramped migrant camps. I argue that the flight of the Pandits was not an unfortunate side-effect of "spontaneous revolt", but the result of a deliberate campaign by Pakistan-sponsored militants and their local collaborators to ethnically cleanse the Valley of its visible Hindu presence.

The chapter also examines the erosion of "Kashmiriyat" as more than just a slogan. I contrast the Valley I knew as a child–where Sufi shrines, temples and gurdwaras coexisted in proximity and everyday life still carried a residue of composite culture—with the Valley of the insurgency years, where fear and majoritarian religious assertion replaced easy familiarity. I show how Islamist slogans, mosque loudspeakers and targeted intimidation gradually narrowed the space for minorities and dissenters, turning a plural society into an increasingly monochrome one. In my view, any honest conversation about the conflict has to start by acknowledging this civilisational loss, rather than reducing everything to unemployment statistics or administrative lapses.

Another strand of this chapter looks at how the Indian state handled the humanitarian fallout. I am sharply critical of both Srinagar and New Delhi for the way they treated Pandit refugees: as temporary problems to be managed, rather than citizens to be restored to their homes with dignity and security. Compensation schemes were announced and forgotten; committees were formed and dissolved; the rhetoric of "return" rarely translated into concrete, sustainable plans. I argue that this failure not only betrayed the Pandits but also weakened India's moral case against Pakistan and separatist groups, because it allowed them to claim that New Delhi itself did not value those who had chosen India and the Indian Constitution.

Chapter 5, therefore, serves as a moral and civilisational anchor for the book. It makes three core claims. First, that the Kashmiri Pandit exodus was a textbook case of targeted religious cleansing, and that any narrative of the conflict that glosses over this fact is fundamentally dishonest. Second, that the erosion of Kashmiriyat was driven not by abstract "alienation" but by a very concrete, Pakistan-fuelled Islamist project that saw pluralism as an obstacle. Third, the Indian state's long neglect of displaced communities and heritage sites in the Valley undermined its own legitimacy and made later assertions of integration harder than they needed to be.

Seen against the backdrop of Article 370's abrogation and the Union Territory reorganisation, this chapter helps explain why many on the right of centre—myself included—came to see full constitutional integration not just as a security imperative, but as a civilisational one. The promise of a different future for Jammu and Kashmir cannot be measured only in incident counts and investment figures; it must also be judged by whether the Valley once again becomes a place where Pandits can live without fear, where pluralism is more than a tourist brochure word, and where the idea of India is visibly at home. Chapter 5 is my attempt to ensure that, amid strategy and statecraft, we do not forget what—and who—was lost.

5.1 FUNDAMENTALIST RAGE IN KASHMIR

December 2002

Much water has flowed under the bridge, and it is a heart-rending incongruity that the Kashmir Valley, long celebrated as Rishivaer or Garden of Rishis, has been in the eye of the storm, with terrorist violence becoming the order of the day. Although the Valley has had a tumultuous history of internal discord and foreign incursions, it has also produced holy men and women who preached a humane faith in the harmonious coexistence of people from different beliefs, and in a God beyond sectarian divisions.

The orthodox Islamic school of thought that eventually found its most dangerous expression in the Taliban originated in the peaceful north-Indian town of Deoband, where Hindus and Muslims co-exist peacefully to the external rhythms of sowing and harvesting. The streets of this holy town are lined with shrines to blue-skinned Hindu gods and cows sacred in Hinduism. In the Kashmiri context, the division is between those who believe in shrines and those who do not. The Islam practised in Kashmir is that propagated by the local Sufi order of Silsila-e-Rishiyan, the Muslim saints of Kashmir, whose progenitor was Sheikh Nooruddin, equally revered by the Valley's Hindus. The Sufis worship at shrines where pre-Islamic practices still survive; the very existence of shrines, as distinct from mosques, is seen by orthodox Islam as non-Islamic. Yet even leaders such as Syed Ali Geelani, who deprecate shrine worship, have had to address congregations at popular shrines like Hazratbal.

Kashmiriyat - the cultural-cum-religious ethos of Kashmir - emerged as an assimilation of influences from Central and West Asia, the Tibetan highlands and the Indian heartland.

Drawing on beliefs, ideas and customs from differing religious convictions and developing its own traditions and way of life, it gave Kashmiris a distinct identity that remains unique to them even today. Kashmir entered a new epoch with the advent of Hinduism in the second century B.C., with the arrival of the Aryans. The beginning of the third millennium B.C. is generally regarded as the period when Buddhist influences took hold, predominantly in Ladakh to the north. Kashmiri intellectuals played a pivotal role in spreading Buddhism to other parts of the world. Even under Buddhist rulers based in the Valley, patronage of Hindu temples and celebration of Hindu festivals continued.

Kashmir was also receptive to the Mahayana school of Buddhism, whose doctrines intertwined with fundamental concepts of Shiva and Shakti. Scholars argue that Buddhism in turn faced a challenge from a rejuvenated Shaivite Hinduism. The Amarnath cave, dedicated to Lord Shiva, symbolises the profound impact of Shaivism on Kashmir's people – an influence that the Buddhist system itself helped foster. It was a form of devotion that emphasized spiritual union between devotee and God, stripped of ritualistic formalism; its growth owed more to popular participation than organised proselytisation. At its height, Kashmir's status as a seat of learning rivalled that of Magadha.

The arrival of Islam, through permeation from Central Asia, Persia and Turkey, saw the decline of Buddhism mainly in the Valley and the conversion of large numbers to the mystic Sufi school. The Valley became a halting-place for caravans travelling in both directions. Syed Ali Hamadani of Hamadan in Persia, an intellectual and Sufi saint, is credited with playing a decisive role in the non-violent spread of Islam in Kashmir. The Kashmiri affinity for Sufi Islam drew on an existing spiritual tradition shaped by Shaivite Hinduism, with its stress on the mystical bond between man and God. It was in the Valley that Muslim ascetics founded the Rishi order – despite the fact that the very notion of a rishi is unknown to

Islam. Hindu saints, for their part, did not shy away from associating with Muslim sages; the common goal of both was self-realisation. Sufism was in part a protest against codified, institutional Islam under sultanates and caliphates, analogous to Shaivite traditions that assigned no special ceremonial role to a priestly class. It also had parallels with tantric rituals that had shaped Kashmiri religious life.

These varied streams formed the basis of Kashmiri society and the evolution of the culture of Kashmiriyat. Long before foreign missionaries arrived, Kashmir already possessed a rich civilisation and an intricate cultural mosaic. Monuments from the Buddhist era such as the Shah-e-Hamadan Mosque on the Jhelum, the Ziyarat Dastgir Sahib in Khanyar and the Ziyarat Nund Rishi at Charar-e-Sharif epitomise the liberal, syncretic version of Islam embraced by Kashmiris. Sufi saints fused monotheistic Trikka (the Kashmiri Shaivite tradition) into the Islamic concept of Tawhid, creating a spiritual way of life at odds with hard-line fundamentalism. The blending of mystic Trikka Shaivism and spiritual Sufism gave rise to the Rishi order, analogous to the Hindu theory of bhakti.

The spread of Islam in this moderate, distinctive form owes much to the Rishis. One such saint was Lal Ded. Born into a Brahmin family in the Pampore area near Srinagar, this fourteenth-century mystic was drawn to spirituality from a young age. She rejected idol worship, sacrifices and other rituals practised by her peers; she made no distinction between Hindu and Muslim, rich and poor. Through her verses, which still echo in the Valley, Lalla-ded preached universal brotherhood and equality before God – a message far removed from the doctrines of fundamentalist Islam.

Popular legends in Kashmir link Lal Ded with both Syed Ali Hamadani and Sheikh Nooruddin Noorani. While her meeting with the former remains unproven, scholars express little doubt about her association with Nund Rishi. Sheikh

Nooruddin, or Nund Rishi, inherited her mantle and is still revered by Muslims and Hindus alike. True spiritualists, their sayings - mostly in simple doggerel - emphasise an ecumenical, inclusive philosophy.

The Rishi tradition is visible in contemporary Kashmir in the post-Namaz recital of Aurade Fathiya - devotional verses in Kashmiri in praise of the Prophet; in the veneration of shrines and tombs of saints and Sufis and the reverence for holy relics; and in the embrace of a tolerant Islamic theology. Kashmiriyat, of which these customs are an essential ingredient, is not confined to modes of worship; it permeates the everyday life of Kashmiris.

The Sufi order, unlike conventional Islamic institutions elsewhere, allows women full agency in shaping their lives; the notion of women as inferior to men is alien to traditional Kashmiri culture. In Kashmir, contrary to orthodox practice, Muslims visiting Hindu temples and Hindus visiting shrines are routine. Muslims follow the Hindu custom of tying threads during the annual Amarnath pilgrimage, and it is Muslim families who traditionally tend the cave. The ethos of coexistence and concord among faiths, and the blending of rituals and practices from different religions, has long underpinned the culture, rejecting fundamentalism and fanaticism. It is the people's departure from this spiritual legacy, bestowed by their saints, that has plunged the Valley into the present scene of carnage.

5.2 CONSTITUENCIES IN EXILE

June 2002

Kashmiri Pandits (KPs), a fundamental constituent of Kashmir's glorious heritage and legacy, find themselves at a crossroads in their twelfth year of exile. More than 8,000 families still languish in refugee camps without adequate sanitation, medical care or education - a condition that can only be described as pitiable. In the past decade over 1,000 KPs have died of snakebites and sunstrokes; the toll from unnatural deaths is put at around 6,000. Psychological trauma and morbidity have inflicted incalculable damage on the community's collective mind, and epidemics have repeatedly broken out in the camps. The National Human Rights Commission (NHRC) has put the number of KPs killed in terrorist violence in Jammu and Kashmir at about 1,200.

The community's political leadership has repeatedly accused the Indian establishment of using KPs as scapegoats. "Our pathetic existence in the camps is being exploited by New Delhi to substantiate its claim over Kashmir in the eyes of the international community," says Moti Kaul of Panun Kashmir. He adds that the community will vehemently oppose any manipulation by governments or vested interests to play fraud on the Constitution and derive mileage from human suffering. "They need us as long as they can exhibit us before the international community for their own political interests," notes another prominent leader. For a community that has made immense contributions to India's growth and has given the country two prime ministers, its present political seclusion has harmed, rather than helped, the democratic process in Jammu and Kashmir.

One rare distinction this minority shares with its estranged Muslim-majority brethren in the Valley is the boycott of both parliamentary and assembly elections in 1996. Community leaders, however, reject the suggestion that this helped separatists, insisting that every Indian has the right to protest and that poll boycotts were a civilised way of conveying their concerns to the nation. Right-wing KP parties now insist that, if they are to participate in the forthcoming assembly elections, the state must first bring perpetrators of what they call "genocide" to justice and create a dispensation for victims of ethno-religious cleansing that reverses the exodus and ensures genuine rehabilitation.

Political analysts believe such maximalist positions have pushed the right-wing groups to the margins within their own community. Moderates, who form an overwhelming majority, say KPs are willing to take part in elections provided a mechanism is devised to guarantee them representation proportionate to their population - something denied in the past. According to the "Charge-sheet on Autonomy" prepared by the Committee to Build Response on Autonomy (CBRA), assembly segments in which KPs could be politically represented were restructured and "fragmented" to reduce them to insignificant minorities within contiguous constituencies, depriving them of the ability to elect their own MLAs. While three KP legislators were returned in 1957, 1962 and 1967, that number fell to one in 1972, 1977, 1983, 1987 and 1996.

A senior Panun Kashmir leader argues there is an urgent need to debate the community's stance on elections, lest it once again be dragged into the process without being taken into confidence. "We feel that a sense of genuine participation can arise only if we are given our due share in the state legislature and in Parliament," he says. The exiled community's most important message to the Election Commission and New Delhi is that they are not "migrants" but Internally Displaced Persons (IDPs) - people forced to flee their homes but remaining in their own country, in line with UN terminology. This would recast their status in exile, contrary to the "ordinary" categorisation used by the Election Commission so far, and would properly frame the question of their participation - or non-participation - in elections.

The postal-ballot system used in the past has proved bogus and open to fraud, with no meaningful checks or counter-checks and ample scope for misuse by political bosses. Two preconditions for postal voting - the voter's freedom to return at will to his or her original residence, and the absence of any abandonment of intent to return - are not met here. These refugees have neither given up their determination to go back, nor are they at liberty to do so as long as terror and violence stalk the Valley. The Election Commission must therefore devise new ways to safeguard their fundamental right to vote outside the present provisions. Agreeing yet again to postal ballots would simply make them tools in the hands of an establishment that failed to protect them when they were prime targets of fundamentalist terror.

Ideally, the electoral process can gain full legitimacy only when exiled KPs return to their original constituencies in a free and fearless atmosphere, resettle in their homes, and vote without coercion to elect their representatives. That prospect, however, is far beyond the present realm of reality. The question, then, is whether KPs should find an optimum way to respond, rather than surrender their right to vote and remain unrepresented in both the assembly and Parliament.

Prof. Shyam Kaul, an eminent writer, notes that KPs are not asking for reservations but for "constituencies in exile" and for recognition of their status in international law. "No communal representation but class representation is demanded," he says, "and they will fight elections as Internally Displaced Persons." Legal expert Prof. T. N. Shalla has also voiced fears that KPs may again remain unrepresented under the current framework and that they feel excluded from the process.

Political and constitutional experts suggest one way out of

the impasse: demand constituencies-in-exile. Under this arrangement, IDPs would be allotted some seats proportionate to the officially registered migrant population, put at over 300,000, enabling them both to stand for office and to elect genuine representatives. This would give them an electoral identity, the first step toward a political identity that, in time, could allow them to negotiate a dignified return to the Valley with full constitutional, economic, religious and other guarantees as enshrined in the Indian Constitution.

5.3 PANDITS IN EXTENDED, UNCERTAIN EXILE

November 2002

We are hard pressed on every side, yet not crushed; We are perplexed, but not in despair; Persecuted, but not forsaken; Struck down, but not destroyed.

CORINTHIANS 4:8-9

Journeys can be long and unsettling - more so when one is forced to live in exile, away from one's roots. It is an excruciating experience, second to none, with a sense of helplessness creeping in day in and day out. You draw on whatever resources are at your disposal to impress upon the policy and decision-makers of the country the need for a meaningful rehabilitation policy for ethnic Kashmiri Pandits. Yet the establishment, sunk in deep slumber, has no ears to heed, leaving people in enforced exile to run from pillar to post.

Kashmiri Pandits (KPs), a fundamental ingredient of Kashmir's glorious heritage and legacy, find themselves at a crossroads in their twelfth year of exile; thousands of families still languish in grotty, tacky refugee camps, devoid of proper sanitation, medical care and education - a state aptly described as pitiable. In the past decade, thousands have succumbed to snakebites and sunstrokes; the toll from unnatural deaths is put at 6,000, with psychological trauma and morbidity inflicting incalculable damage on the community's "collective mind."

This ethnic community has its erudite members spread across the length and breadth of the country, earning livelihoods for their families, often as the sole breadwinners. Thank God education has always been our foremost priority; otherwise, we might have been reduced to begging on the streets to survive. Yet, stuck in a rut, there are still thousands of hapless souls – with tears of excruciating pain and pangs – who, even after more than a decade in exile, fade away in the camps and wait for better times to arrive.

It is regrettable that, despite a notable track record in India's growth and development, the original inhabitants of Kashmir see themselves discriminated against, while primacy is given to the perceived travails of the Muslim majority in the Valley. That appears to be the only priority; everything else is secondary and inconsequential. The establishment seems to have a freewheeling attitude towards this minority.

The Bharatiya Janata Party (BJP), a party with (no) difference, which long advocated the "complete" integration of the Valley with the Indian Union and decried its special status as the primary cause of alienation, has dropped these core issues; its only apparent priority now, despite internal dissent, is to back the Abdullahs to the hilt. The party even seems to forget the sacrifice of its founder-president, Syama Prasad Mookerjee, who died under mysterious circumstances in Srinagar while protesting against Jammu and Kashmir's special status.

Despite fervent appeals from all quarters to exercise the franchise in the larger national interest, Pandits chose to shun the electoral process, underscoring the apathy of political parties. Right-wing Pandit groups, including Panun Kashmir, ensured a near-total boycott, arguing that elections are meaningless when the establishment has consistently ignored their aspirations – including the demand for "Internally Displaced Persons" (IDP) status as recognised by UN bodies.

To rub salt into their wounds, Minister of State for Home I. D. Swami chose the worst possible time – just before elections – to unveil a much-touted package for KPs that turned out to be such a crude parody that it was flatly rejected by the community. A cursory look at the scheme framed by the Home Ministry was enough to show it was a mere gambit by

New Delhi to entice Pandits into participation – a ploy that badly backfired.

The political leadership of this minority has repeatedly accused the Indian establishment of using KPs as scapegoats and transgressing the limits of decency. Their pathetic existence in camps is exploited by New Delhi to bolster its claim over Kashmir before the international community, they allege, denouncing such moves as manipulation by governments and vested state interests to play fraud on the Constitution and extract mileage from human suffering.

The National Conference, for all its vaunted history, did nothing during its tenure to alleviate Pandit hardship. Jammu, the winter capital, and nearby Udhampur host large Pandit populations that have borne the brunt of an unresponsive administration. Their journey in exile continues; decent housing and basic amenities recede further into the realm of daydream with each passing day.

A close-knit community proud of its distinctive culture is rapidly losing hope of preserving its identity as an ethnic minority, an issue very close to its heart. Pandits also harbour deep resentment against India's intellectual establishment for what they see as its partisan, unforgivable silence over their ethnic cleansing at the hands of jihadi elements. They are distressed by the way national media highlighted the suffering of the Muslim minority in Gujarat while virtually ignoring similar horrors in the early 1990s, when Pandits were persecuted in the Valley. Many conclude that, because Pandits do not constitute a substantial vote bank, both electronic and print media have half-informed the country about the truth, reflecting the poor mindset they epitomise.

This journey of misery has gone on far too long. There is an urgent need for measures at both national and regional levels to end this prolonged nightmare. Initiating direct talks with Pandit representatives is essential to restoring their due dignity as proud citizens of this country. Watching events with bated breath, these refugees have neither abandoned their intent to return to their homeland nor are they free to do so while terror and violence haunt the Valley. The prejudice meted out to these fellow countrymen must end - the sooner, the better.

5.4 KASHMIR PANDITS AND THE 'HEALING TOUCH'

January 2003

New Delhi went ecstatic over the successful October 2002 elections in troubled Jammu & Kashmir, and rightly so: for once, its stand on Kashmir was vindicated by the international community in a way not seen before. The widespread appreciation and accolades for reviving democratic norms in the Valley were a severe setback for Islamabad, which has since been under pressure to rethink its Kashmir policy. To say that New Delhi's position on Kashmir has been strengthened is merely to state the obvious.

Yet it is imperative that New Delhi, which has incessantly shied away from framing a meaningful policy to alleviate the suffering of 3.5 lakh internally displaced Kashmiri Pandits, now accept responsibility for giving them just treatment, as envisaged in various UN conventions and guidelines (including those of UNHCR). India is a signatory to the UN Guiding Principles on Internal Displacement, but has shown scant interest in applying them to Kashmiri Pandits. Why should it, some might ask, when KPs - unlike their counterparts in Gujarat - do not constitute a sizeable vote-bank? The entire nation can generate a hullabaloo over riot victims in Gujarat, yet shy away from debating the plight of KPs, which remains inconsequential in political terms. A deeply polarised discourse framed exclusively in Hindu-majority/Muslim-minority terms has left India's intellectual class unable to confront the reality that Kashmiri Pandits are, at the very least, a minority in Muslim-majority Jammu and Kashmir, even though they belong to a Hindu-majority country.

Worldwide, there are some 25 million internally displaced persons (IDPs). In India, conflict-induced displacement affects more than half a million people, concentrated mainly in Kashmir and the Northeast. Armed conflict, internal strife and systematic human-rights violations are widely recognised as the key drivers forcing millions from their homes while they remain within their own borders, unlike refugees who cross frontiers and benefit from long-established international protection regimes. Those uprooted but still inside their country often find themselves at the mercy of "their own" state, which may lack predictable support structures; internal displacement has thus assumed dimensions requiring urgent attention if governments are not to be accused of neglecting basic humanitarian and security obligations towards their own citizens.

Systematic human-rights violations against KPs have been documented before national and international bodies. Yet, beyond passing references in their reports, most human-rights organisations have avoided the kind of proactive stance they took in Gujarat, where they forcefully pressed for accountability. Ashwani Kumar Chrungoo, a KP human-rights activist, has rendered yeoman's service in highlighting abuses against Pandits, but his efforts have run up against the apathy of institutions like the National Human Rights Commission (NHRC) and their apparent "selective" application of human-rights principles.

The NHRC has described crimes against KPs as "stark and tragic" and deserving the strongest condemnation, and its observations on submissions made by Chrungoo were, on paper, encouraging. Yet it stopped short of issuing strong strictures against the political-administrative set-up that presided over the worst atrocities, and did not fix responsibility for the violations. The Commission also declined to term the selective killing of Pandits as "genocide", preferring phrases such as "acts akin to genocide" and "genocide-type design" to describe the mindset of the Islamist extremists behind the ethnic cleansing. It likewise failed to grapple fully with the denial of fundamental rights guaranteed to KPs under Articles 19 and 21 of the Constitution.

By contrast, the NHRC played a highly proactive role after the Gujarat riots, issuing scathing strictures against both state and central governments for their failure to protect Muslim minorities. One is left to wonder whether, had the Commission adopted a similar posture in the Kashmiri context, the trajectory of KP suffering might have been different and some "healing touch" applied long ago. Instead, New Delhi has repeatedly ducked the task of formulating serious policies and programmes for IDPs, preferring a criminal silence that has prolonged the agony of this exiled community.

UNHCR does not directly work with IDPs in India because such involvement requires, among other things, the consent of the host government - something New Delhi has withheld despite repeated offers of help, including on drafting national refugee legislation. India's stance betrays a lack of consensus at the decision-making level, which, in turn, has worsened conditions for IDPs over time. The official claim that the rights restated in the Guiding Principles are already covered by the Constitution, and that courts and procedures suffice to protect the displaced, rings hollow: if these mechanisms were truly effective, justice would by now have been done to KPs and their condition would have improved, not deteriorated.

"India is no Somalia or Rwanda" is one of the stock arguments New Delhi cites to explain its reluctance to seek or accept international assistance for IDPs. Fair enough - but if that is so, it must devise and implement robust domestic mechanisms to deliver justice to victims of conflict-induced displacement. In the absence of such policies, people in this predicament will continue to suffer because of a misplaced sense of pride. In the case of KPs, New Delhi should, at the very least, begin crafting a coherent framework covering non-discrimination, movement-related rights, physical protection and the special needs of IDPs.

It is worth recalling Amnesty International's August 1997 report, which urged "persons learned in law, politicians mindful of the consequences, and human rights activists not ignorant of what has happened in Kashmir" to focus their attention on long-pending violations against the Pandit minority and, instead of maintaining a "strategic silence", to suggest dispassionately how their issues of genocide, ethnic cleansing and exile can be addressed to their satisfaction by "this colossal nation – that is India." Since then, substantial groundwork has been done by KPs in the diaspora, particularly in the US and UK. Congressman Frank Pallone has been at the forefront of efforts to highlight their plight, while organisations like the Indo-American Kashmir Forum and Kashmir News Network have pressed for redress within the UN's framework for IDPs.

Against this demeaning backdrop, the most plausible option left to Pandits, in the author's view, may be to approach the International Court of Justice. New Delhi's continued apathy – even under a right-wing Hindu government – has left them with little choice but to contemplate legal action against their own state in an international tribunal, however painful that may be. To claim that India bears no responsibility for their fate would be to wilfully ignore the obvious.

CHAPTER 6: PEACE RESOLUTIONS AND PARTITION FANTASIES

In this chapter, I step back from the immediacy of elections, terror attacks and daily governance to examine the larger diplomatic and legal frames that have long surrounded the Kashmir question. Here, I revisit the United Nations resolutions, the many so-called peace initiatives, and the recurring proposals to "partition" or "internationalise" Jammu and Kashmir. My argument is that by 2002-2003, these frameworks had become less a roadmap for peace and more a set of illusions that Pakistan and parts of the international community clung to avoid facing hard realities.

I begin with the UN Security Council resolutions of 1948-1951, which Pakistan still cites as if they were timeless scripture. I walk through what those resolutions actually said, and more importantly, the conditions they laid down: Pakistan was to withdraw its tribesmen and nationals, stop sending fighters and material aid into the state, and fully demilitarise the areas it occupied before any plebiscite could even be considered. India, for its part, signalled readiness for a UN-supervised vote if and only if those preconditions were met. They never were. By 2002, more than half a century later, Pakistan had not withdrawn its forces, had not dismantled "Azad Kashmir" militias, and had in fact formalised control over parts of the territory it seized in 1947-48. In my reading, the UN resolutions had therefore become a dead letter—not because India "ran away" from them, but because Pakistan never fulfilled the first, non-negotiable steps.

The next set of essays dissects what passed for "peace

processes" in the early 2000s. I examine New Delhi's outreach to the All Parties Hurriyat Conference (Hurriyat Conference), the appointment of N.N. Vohra as the Centre's interlocutor in 2003, and the atmospherics around bus services, ceasefire announcements and Track-II dialogues. My critique is not of talking per se; it is of talking in a way that rewarded intransigence and sidelined those who had actually participated in the democratic process. Separatist leaders who had called for boycotts and implicitly endorsed violence found themselves courted, while elected representatives and ordinary voters were treated as background scenery. In parallel, Pakistan used every "peace moment" to seek moral equivalence, insisting that its sponsorship of jihad was the mirror image of India's security presence.

I then turn to partition and joint-management proposals: ideas that surface regularly in international think-tank reports and expatriate drawing rooms. Some of these can be traced back to Owen Dixon's mid-twentieth-century suggestions; others are newer maps that carve up Jammu and Kashmir along religious or regional lines, dress it up as "creative solutions", and then expect Indians and Kashmiris to treat them as serious options. In these essays, I argue that most such plans share three flaws. First, they reduce living regions and communities to cartographic abstractions. Second, they reward Pakistan's aggression by formalising gains made through invasion and proxy war. Third, they ignore the rights and traumas of groups like the Pandits, Ladakhis and large segments of Jammu who have already paid a high price for betting on the Indian Union.

Chapter 6 makes four core points. First, that the UN resolutions, when read honestly and in sequence, cannot be used today as a stick to beat India with, because their core preconditions were never met by Pakistan and the ground realities they presupposed have been irrevocably altered. Second, that peace processes which elevate separatists and external actors while sidelining those committed to the Constitution are inherently unstable and morally perverse. Third, that partition and quasi-protectorate schemes—whether under the UN, joint Indo-Pak sovereignty, or some other flag—are dangerous fantasies that ignore both history and the popular will in key regions. And fourth, that for India, the only sustainable framework is one that treats Jammu and Kashmir as an integral part of the Union, to be managed through democratic politics, firm security policy and constitutional clarity—not through perpetual bargaining over status.

Seen from the post-2019 landscape—after Article 370's abrogation, the Union Territory reorganisation, the formal burial of any "special status" fiction, and the closing of the door on third-party mediation—this chapter reads as a bridge between past illusions and present clarity. The arguments I advanced in 2002-2003 in newspaper columns and policy essays now sit much closer to India's official line: that there will be no plebiscite, no re-opening of accession, no external role in our internal reorganisation, and no reward for Pakistan's decades-long jihad. If the earlier chapters explain why the Indian state had to rethink its security and constitutional posture, Chapter 6 explains why it also had to shed the diplomatic baggage of half-remembered resolutions and romanticised peace processes.

6.1 UNITED NATIONS RESOLUTIONS AND KASHMIR

December 2002

First, they ignore you, then they laugh at you, then they fight you, then you win.

Mahatma Gandhi

New Delhi wishes to deal with the Kashmiris within a domestic framework and to hold any talks with Pakistan independently of, and after, dialogue with Kashmiri representatives. India's reluctance to alter this policy is reinforced by its belief that Pakistan would play the spoiler if New Delhi embarked on any bold initiative towards the Kashmiris. Formally, however, Islamabad still invokes the 1949 UN resolutions and their call for a plebiscite in which Kashmiris choose between India and Pakistan. Since early 2001, Pakistani spokesmen have shifted tack, suggesting that Pakistan might accept any resolution "acceptable to the Kashmiris."

Taken at face value, the very UN resolutions to which Pakistan swears allegiance explicitly acknowledged the legality of Jammu & Kashmir's accession to India and gave rise to the term "Pakistan-occupied Kashmir" (Pakistan- occupied Kashmir). India approached the UN on 1 January 1948, complaining of Pakistani aggression against the state of Jammu and Kashmir and requesting that the Security Council call upon Pakistan "to immediately stop" what New Delhi described as aggression. Earlier, on 3 December 1947, Nehru had written to Sheikh Abdullah that Kashmir had become to him a symbol of India's basic conflict and that on its decision "depends not only the future of Kashmir but the future of Pakistan and, to a considerable extent, the future of India."

On 20 January 1948, the Security Council set up a

three-member commission, later expanded to five, and on 21 April 1948 outlined the details of a plebiscitary solution. A plebiscite administrator, to be nominated by the UN Secretary-General, was to act as an officer of the State of Jammu and Kashmir and "have authority to nominate his assistants ... and to draft regulations governing the plebiscite," with such nominees formally appointed and such regulations formally promulgated by the state government. This amounted to clear recognition of the legality of accession, India's external sovereignty over Jammu and Kashmir and the legal authority of the state government.

When the commission arrived in Pakistan in July, it learnt that three brigades of regular Pakistani troops had been fighting in Kashmir since May. On 15 July 1948, Mountbatten wrote from London to Nehru that, with such evidence, the commission could produce a report "reasonably favourable" to India and "resolve the tangle" in a manner acceptable to New Delhi. Yet the commission glossed over these incursions, provoking sharp protests from India. On 16 February 1948, Nehru wrote to Vijaya Lakshmi Pandit that he "could not imagine" the Security Council behaving in so "trivial and partisan" a manner, adding that "the US and Britain have played dirty, Britain being the chief actor behind the scenes."

Under the 13 August 1948 UNCIP resolution, Pakistan was required to withdraw its tribesmen and nationals who had entered Jammu and Kashmir for fighting purposes, while India was to withdraw "the bulk" of its forces, retaining only enough to assist local authorities in maintaining law and order. The existence of the Jammu and Kashmir government was explicitly recognised, as was its accession to India and India's assumption of external sovereignty; the government of the state was to safeguard law and order and ensure that human and political rights were respected. In stark contrast, the resolution provided that any territory evacuated by Pakistani troops would be "administered by the local authorities under the supervision of the commission," with no comparable external supervision envisaged for the Indian-administered part. India accepted the resolution; Pakistan did not. Both sides later accepted clarificatory proposals offered on 11 December 1948.

A memorandum of 14 January 1949 by the Committee on India and Pakistan made clear that if Pakistan refused the plebiscite proposals, or accepted them without implementing the first two articles of the 13 August resolution, India would be under no obligation to proceed. Pakistan, therefore, remained bound to vacate the territory it had seized in Jammu and Kashmir by armed aggression. Frustrated by Islamabad's persistent attempts to scuttle the process, India in December 1950 rejected further UN mediation, with Nehru telling the world body that "the only way to solve it is for India and Pakistan to know that the burden is upon them and no one else." New Delhi particularly bristled at draft provisions envisaging supersession of the Kashmiri government and possible entry of foreign troops, given the evidence of Pakistani aggression.

From 1952 onwards, the Soviet Union repeatedly endorsed India's legal position. On 17 January 1952, Ambassador Jacob Malik condemned the Anglo-American stance and argued that Kashmir's status should be determined by a constituent assembly "democratically elected by the Kashmiri people." On 23 December 1952, Valerian Zorin again stressed that settlement could be achieved by having a democratically elected constituent assembly decide the state's status. On 19 February 1957, Arkady Sobolev declared that the Kashmir question had "in actual fact already been settled in essence by the people of Kashmir themselves, who consider their territory an integral part of the Republic of India," and opposed any UN provisions that ignored this reality. On 4 May 1962, Platon Morozov noted that a plebiscite could have taken place only if Pakistan had first withdrawn its troops; as this precondition was never met, "the question of holding it has lapsed."

Meanwhile, Pakistan steadily violated the very resolutions it invoked. On 21 June 1952, it imposed a new regime in Pakistan-occupied Kashmir, and the rules of business adopted on 28 October declared that the "president" of Azad Kashmir held office at the pleasure of the All-Jammu and Kashmir Muslim Conference, as recognised by Pakistan's Ministry of Kashmir Affairs. Islamabad never withdrew its forces or infiltrators. Instead, it constructed airfields and imposed full civilian and military control while claiming the territory as "Azad Kashmir". To secure Chinese support, it handed over 4,853 sq. km of the Shaksgam Valley to Beijing in 1963, undermining Jammu and Kashmir's territorial integrity, while China itself occupied Aksai Chin - about 19 per cent of the state. Later, through constitutional amendment, Pakistan effectively incorporated the "Northern Areas" into its territory and altered Pakistan- occupied Kashmir's demography by settling Punjabi ex-servicemen and Afghan migrants, further eroding the basis for any meaningful plebiscite.

Legally, Jammu and Kashmir's accession to India was incontestable, yet India still agreed to a plebiscite in 1948. The prime factors that have since rendered such a vote impossible are Pakistan's annexation and militarisation of Pakistan- occupied Kashmir, its refusal to withdraw forces from occupied areas and its broader policies towards the rest of the state. As Nehru wrote to Sheikh Abdullah on 25 August 1952, Pakistan's rulers "are like someone riding a bicycle. They feel that the moment they return to normalcy, the bicycle stops and they fall."

In this light, the All Parties Hurriyat Conference and company - Islamabad's political face in Kashmir - continue to demand implementation of UN resolutions, a stance that remains a major stumbling block to future negotiations with New Delhi. But this is something no Indian government, regardless of party, will ever accept. It is time for separatist leaders to be realistic and practical: when official talks eventually begin, they must enter with an open mind, not with pre-packaged demands that have long since been consigned to the historical dustbin - not by India, but by their own benefactor, Pakistan.

6.2 KASHMIR: TRYST WITH DESTINY

March 2003

This happens to be India's 56th year of independence - a landmark, although fifty-six years is a very short epoch in a nation's history, especially when our civilisation dates back over eight thousand years. A multi-religious, multi-ethnic polity like India, which has never had a formal communal power-sharing arrangement, might well have fragmented long ago; that it is alive and functioning 56 years after birth is no mean achievement.

Barely two months after India was born, Indian troops were flown to Srinagar on the morning of 27 October, just in time to prevent the complete siege of the city and thwart Pakistan's plan to proclaim accession after capturing it. Thus began the era of claims and counter-claims over Kashmir - 56 years of dispute that has already produced four wars in the subcontinent (if Kargil is included). Looking back over the historical record is daunting, but it also throws up some astounding and uncomfortable facts. Certain aspects are so subtle that one hesitates to offer personal judgements; yet the reality is that grave mistakes were made, which helped sow today's turmoil.

In 1931, Sheikh Abdullah founded the Muslim Conference to mobilise Kashmiri Muslims against Dogra rule. In later years, he was attracted by Pandit Nehru's liberalism and the Indian National Congress's secular platform, left the Muslim Conference and formed the National Conference as a secular party for all Kashmiris. In response to the Quit India movement, he launched the Quit Kashmir movement against Maharaja Hari Singh. It bears recalling that Hari Singh's father, Raja Gulab Singh, had "purchased" Jammu and Kashmir from the British for 75 lakh rupees after the first Anglo-Sikh war in 1846; when he entered Srinagar that

November, a long "reign of terror" against Kashmiri Muslims is widely believed to have begun, even as Kashmiri Pandits, by virtue of their education, were given high administrative posts.

Under Maharaja Pratap Singh (1894–1925), conditions deteriorated further, with the British encouraging communal thinking among Kashmir's Muslims; by 1931, the state saw its first major communal clash. Muslim communalism was championed by the Muslim Conference. In 1946, the Maharaja jailed Sheikh Abdullah for 20 years for leading a revolt against his throne. On 29 September 1947, "Sher-e-Kashmir" was released at Nehru's instance; after his release, he campaigned for democratic rights and, in public at least, did not dwell on accession.

On 16 September 1947, Nehru told the press that Partition was a short-term political fix that could not override cultural affinities and economic compulsions, that India bore no ill-will towards Pakistan, and that once turmoil ended, the two states might, by the free will of their peoples, even unite. That hope was shattered on the night of 24 October, when Delhi learnt that organised tribal raiders from Pakistan had entered the Valley and were advancing on Srinagar. When Kashmiri Prime Minister Ramchand Kak sought Indian troops the next day, Nehru initially expressed helplessness and was only persuaded by Abdullah and Sardar Patel to agree.

Contrary to popular belief, Nehru's Kashmir decisions were not taken in romantic isolation, even though his love for the mountains is well-known. At a Defence Committee meeting on 26 October, Mountbatten persuaded both Nehru and Patel to insist on formal accession as a precondition for military aid, coupled with an offer of a plebiscite after law and order was restored. On 27 October, once Kashmir's accession was accepted, Indian troops were airlifted just in time to save Srinagar and frustrate what was seen as Pakistan's plan to capture the city and let "Jinnah makes a triumphal entry." That same day, Nehru wrote to Abdullah: "I heard today that our troops had reached Srinagar ... We have taken the plunge, and we shall swim across to the other shore."

Meanwhile, the raiders left pools of blood in their wake, slaughtering Sikhs and Hindus, committing mass rapes, arson and looting. The efforts of ordinary Muslims in general and National Conference cadres in particular to shelter Hindus and Sikhs at great personal risk were praiseworthy. In a 1947 secret note to the Government of India, Ram Manohar Lohia recorded that between 1887 and 1947 the Pandit population had fallen from one lakh to 80,000 while the Muslim population had risen from five lakh to twenty lakh – a demographic shift that left minorities increasingly marginalised and voiceless in state politics.

Seeing no easy solution, Nehru remained unwilling to compromise. On 3 December 1947, he wrote to Abdullah that Kashmir had become a symbol of India's basic conflict and that on its outcome "depends not only the future of Kashmir but the future of Pakistan and to a considerable extent the future of India." Eventually, on Lord Mountbatten's advice, he agreed to refer the matter to the United Nations – but strictly based on Indian complaints under Article 35 of the UN Charter, seeking only vacation of Pakistani aggression. Nehru would later regret this historic step.

India's case suffered once the issue went to the Security Council. Pakistan not only refuted the charges but counter-attacked, accusing India of hostility. UN decisions were perceived in Delhi as one-sided and biased. British delegate Philip Noel-Baker assured the Council, and India, that Pakistan was not assisting the raiders – a stance Nehru denounced in a 16 February 1948 letter to Vijaya Lakshmi Pandit as "trivial and partisan", adding that "the US and Britain have played a dirty game, Britain being the chief actor behind the scenes." British duplicity, backed by Washington, continued to shape policy in the region even after India's independence.

When the UN commission finally arrived in Pakistan in July 1948, it was informed that three brigades of regular Pakistani troops had been fighting in Kashmir since May. Mountbatten wrote to Nehru on 15 July that, with such evidence, the commission could produce a report "reasonably favourable" to India. Nevertheless, the 13 August 1948 resolution merely called for a ceasefire and phased withdrawals: Pakistan was to pull out its troops, nationals and tribesmen; India was then to withdraw the bulk of her forces; and a plebiscite would determine the state's future. By May 1949, with no real progress, the commission advanced new proposals so biased that Nehru rejected them outright.

In December 1950, India turned down further UN mediation. "The only way to solve it is for India and Pakistan to know that the burden is upon them and no one else," Nehru wrote. He was alarmed by draft provisions condemning the convening of the Kashmiri constituent assembly, providing for the supersession of the state government, and even contemplating foreign troops in Kashmir. In a 2 June 1950 letter to Vijaya Lakshmi Pandit he warned that, if Pakistan's communal approach prevailed in Kashmir, it would not only be a tragedy for the state but would "upset the whole scheme of things in India", adding that the British and Americans were "skating merrily on this very thin ice over the deep ocean" while accusing India of intransigence.

By August 1952, Nehru could write in a note for Abdullah that "the Government of Pakistan is like someone riding a bicycle. They feel that the moment they return to normalcy, the bicycle stops, and they fall down." His Kashmir policy, from the start, was woven around one man - Sheikh Mohammad Abdullah. The National Conference's sweeping victory in elections to the constituent assembly made Nehru even more optimistic about a plebiscite, and he took up the issue with Abdullah. At the UN, however, British-sponsored draft resolutions still ignored India's position and past commitments, drawing sharp criticism from the Soviet Union. Despite India's protests, one such resolution passed; Nehru promptly rejected it in toto.

On the domestic front, Abdullah's shifting attitude became a major concern. It was his popularity that had underpinned Nehru's confidence when ordering prompt military action in 1947. "The only person who can deliver the goods in Kashmir is Abdullah... I have a high opinion [of him]... He may make any number of mistakes in minor matters...," Nehru wrote to the Maharaja on 13 November 1947. Over time, however, Abdullah's intentions came into question; Nehru was quietly warned that the Sheikh harboured long-standing ideas of an independent Kashmir and was cultivating Anglo-American contacts.

Sardar Patel strongly objected when, in September 1948, Abdullah claimed that certain people in India were prepared to "surrender" Kashmir to Pakistan. Abdullah remained unapologetic, and his divergence from Nehru's line became more pronounced. Even after accession, he flirted with the idea of an "independent Kashmir". His dismissal and imprisonment in August 1953 were the logical culmination of his Anglo-American links and separatist leanings. It was not until the 1975 Indira–Sheikh accord that he finally abandoned the independence dream, by which time serious damage had been done, with pro-Pakistan forces gaining ground in a vacuum created by his inability to translate his own vision into reality.

6.3 R&AW: KASHMIR AND BEYOND

July 2002

Research and Analysis Wing, commonly known by its acronym R&AW or simply RAW, is formally an external intelligence agency but is also known to run domestic operations, especially in Indian states where separatist or secessionist movements are strong. Formed in 1968, RAW has had mixed success. Its high point was during the liberation of Bangladesh, when it played a major role in ensuring that Sheikh Mujibur Rahman's Mukti Bahini movement succeeded. As one analyst notes, Indian sources have put on record how, well before 1971, RAW had established a separatist network through "cells" inside East Pakistan and training camps in adjoining Indian territory; the Mukti Bahini were thus in place organisationally to exploit the 1971 crisis, sabotage communication lines and facilitate the Indian Army's entry at the "right" time, with RAW agents providing intelligence and conducting unconventional guerrilla acts against Pakistani forces.

By contrast, its Sri Lanka policy is widely viewed as one of RAW's biggest setbacks. The fact that "Voice of America" once referred to the LTTE as "Indian Contra rebels" speaks volumes about the depth of Indian intelligence involvement and who Prabhakaran's early mentors were before he turned on them. According to Rohan Gunaratna in Indian Intervention in Sri Lanka, RAW waged a secret war from 1983 so that, by the time Sri Lankan forces launched a major offensive in 1987, New Delhi had already ensured the Tamils were well-supplied and able to carry out terrorist acts that brought the war closer to Colombo.

RAW has had limited success in Nepal, Bhutan and even the Maldives, which it hoped to use as a base for anti-Sri Lanka operations. One analyst argues that the ethnic crisis in

Bhutan, led by people of Nepali origin, was aggravated by RAW to turn the political crisis to India's advantage, and that in Nepal, India has consistently intervened in this landlocked Hindu kingdom's politics by backing pro-India politicians, leveraging Kathmandu's economic dependence on India.

Unlike its Pakistani counterpart, RAW has had a limited role in domestic politics and is not systematically used for espionage against internal political opponents, as the ISI has been in Pakistan. RAW maintains a comparatively low profile; little is known about its structure beyond the fact that its chief reports directly to the prime minister.

On Pakistani soil, it has had only moderate operational success. It has supported separatist and secessionist movements, but has not been able to sustain them long enough to cause the kind of lasting damage ISI has caused in Kashmir. Pakistan has repeatedly accused RAW of sponsoring sabotage in Punjab, supporting the Seraiki movement, funding its activities and even organising an international Seraiki conference in New Delhi in 1993.

One senior analyst notes that, before the Soviet intervention in Afghanistan changed the Pakistan–Afghanistan equation, RAW tried to nurture the Pakhtunistan issue clandestinely while New Delhi courted elements of the NWFP political elite. When Baloch grievances flared after Z. A. Bhutto dismissed that province's elected government, RAW is said to have moved quickly to play up Punjabi dominance. While the Baloch insurgency had local roots, it was allegedly sustained with external aid funnelled via Afghanistan, with RAW's "trademark" visible along that route.

RAW's role first attracted serious notice in the late 1960s when it reportedly began training separatists in camps along the East Pakistan border. Its main successes inside Pakistan were recorded after the Soviet invasion of Afghanistan. It is alleged that RAW, in collusion with Afghan intelligence and the KGB, inflicted serious damage on the mujahideen movement through covert operations. As Ikram Sehgal has written, the Kabul regime, backed by KGB, KHAD and RAW, responded to Pakistan's support for the mujahideen with bombings in major Pakistani cities, targeting markets, transport and other soft nodes – "a coward's way" of inflicting maximum harm on non-combatants – while groups like Al-Zulfikar were trained and funded by KHAD and RAW, under KGB coordination, to export terrorism to their governments' perceived enemies.

Former RAW chief A. S. Dulat, now in the Prime Minister's Office, is widely regarded as the main architect of the agency's operations in Kashmir. Beyond its conventional tasks – tracking militant leadership and networks – RAW is seen to have gradually assumed a political role in the Valley, mirroring the ISI's role in Pakistan. Dr Bhaskar Kasturi, in "Notes on the Hizbul Mujahideen and the Indian Intelligence", writes that Dulat, who handled Kashmir for years in the Intelligence Bureau, enjoyed the ear of everyone from the prime minister to Jammu and Kashmir Chief Minister Farooq Abdullah, and that his views were rarely questioned. The one public exception came when he accompanied Brajesh Mishra to Srinagar for talks with Hurriyat leaders, and Hurriyat chief Abdul Ghani Bhat asked him to leave the room.

Farooq Abdullah himself is often cited as evidence of Dulat's influence; many stories credit Dulat with playing a key role in Farooq's return to the chief ministership a few years earlier. On this reading, the unilateral "ceasefire" initiative of the Hizbul Mujahideen period is seen as a RAW operation to penetrate and split the outfit, a move that in practice, only strengthened Farooq, especially once the government that had freed Hurriyat leaders with great fanfare seemed to turn its back on them. Dulat's proximity to Abdullah as RAW chief is well-known; his successor, Vikram Sood, has broadly followed the agenda set by his predecessor.

The ISI has always had a pronounced political dimension, and its role in manipulating political outcomes in Pakistan is well documented. RAW has now assumed a comparable role in Kashmir, where "political cells" have reportedly been set up involving moderate separatists, NRI Kashmiris (including Pandits) and counter-insurgents, intending to influence the political trajectory of the conflict.

The most prominent counter-insurgent formation was Ikhwan-ul-Musalmeen, led by Jamsheed Shirazi alias Kuka Parrey, now a sitting MLA. With backing from Indian security forces, he played a major role in wresting control of parts of South Kashmir from Pakistan-sponsored separatists. Yet, in keeping with precedent, New Delhi chose not to carry this counter-insurgency strategy to its logical conclusion, deciding instead that the state would be safer in the hands of the "prodigal son", Farooq Abdullah. Had it stuck with the earlier policy, some argue, outcomes might have been different. After returning to power, Abdullah ensured that assistance to these counter-insurgent groups was cut off, enabling Pakistan-backed militants systematically to eliminate their leaders.

The Hurriyat Conference, the political face of the Pakistan-backed separatist movement, has been riven by factionalism frequently attributed to Indian intelligence activity. New Delhi's policy towards Hurriyat has oscillated between "stick and carrot": an initial crackdown saw frontline leaders jailed across India, partly to marginalise separatists and restore Farooq Abdullah's centrality. Later, with the arrival of foreign mercenaries adding a new dimension to the insurgency, Delhi shifted tack and reportedly sought tacit understandings with "moderate" Hurriyat leaders, paving the way for their release and eventual "peace talks". K. C. Pant's appointment as the government's chief interlocutor on Kashmir followed this groundwork, in which RAW is believed to have played an instrumental role.

Over time, therefore, RAW concentrated on building political cells inside and outside Kashmir to explore prospects for reviving a mass-based political process. But the experiment soon ran into trouble: many separatist leaders turned out to be double agents playing both sides and, contrary to expectations, they failed to deliver.

Dr Bidanda M. Chengappa of IDSA, in his typology of intelligence agencies, distinguishes between (a) a bureau of domestic intelligence - charter-bound, focused on information-gathering and prosecution and not on aggressive political operations; (b) political police - relatively autonomous, insulated from legislative and judicial scrutiny, close to ruling elites and empowered to conduct political operations against opponents; and (c) an independent security state - free of effective external control, with goals determined by agency officials that may diverge from those of elected leaders.

In that context, the million-dollar question is whether our own intelligence agency is, in Kashmir, edging towards the same kind of role that the ISI plays across Pakistan - and, if so, what that means for democratic accountability and for any genuine political resolution of the conflict.

6.4 U.S, INDIA AND PAKISTAN: THE TANTALISING TRIANGLE

November 2002

One of the greatest intrinsic merits India exhibited during the Cold War was its ability to remain non-aligned, a principle that formed the core of our foreign policy until recently. A multi-religious, multi-ethnic country that never institutionalised communal power-sharing might easily have slipped into blocs; instead, it preserved strategic autonomy. Under the BJP-led government, however, that legacy has been substantially undone, to the point where India is increasingly seen as playing second fiddle to the United States, much like Great Britain - a precedent no previous regime, Congress or otherwise, had seriously contemplated.

With the bipolar world disappearing after the break-up of the USSR, the United States emerged as the lone superpower and has, in many eyes, assumed quasi-imperial dimensions, arm-twisting developing states like India to serve its own regional designs. Washington has often shown that it is less the protector of democracy abroad than an imperial muscle willing to "launder" discredited juntas when convenient, with the World Bank and IMF providing discretionary support to regimes that further US interests. New Delhi has succumbed to this pressure and allowed its foreign policy to be shaped by Washington and its network of influential officials. Ambassador Robert Blackwill, for instance, while certifying the fairness of the Kashmir elections, has continued to press India to align its South Asian policies with US preferences. Despite ritual denials of "mediation" on Kashmir, New Delhi has struggled to explain why it lacks a composite, self-driven policy on the issue.

Why should the US instruct us on our next diplomatic

steps with Islamabad? It was virtually pre-ordained – in line with Washington's script – that India, after the Kashmir polls, would de-escalate. It was common knowledge in diplomatic circles that New Delhi would move to "create a conducive atmosphere" for talks with Pakistan despite there being no credible evidence that Islamabad had addressed India's core concerns. Pakistan continues to shelter wanted fugitives, has not dismantled terror camps in Pakistan-occupied Kashmir, and still aids and abets militants in Jammu and Kashmir. What has actually changed on the ground to justify New Delhi's gestures?

India has put on a brave face while undoing the measures adopted after the December 2001 Parliament attack. The decision to pull back troops from the border has been vigorously defended, but has not found wide acceptance in political or intellectual circles. There are already indications that Track-II diplomacy will soon resume, laying the groundwork for another summit with Pakistan, possibly in January. The failure of the Agra summit is widely attributed to inadequate preparatory work, and both sides now appear anxious to avoid a repeat by putting more spadework into any future dialogue.

What remains incongruous is India's lack of nerve or resolve in confronting cross-border terrorism orchestrated by Pakistan's ISI. We have enacted tough laws like POTA, yet have failed to prevent the spread of terror networks into new regions, let alone stamp them out in long-affected areas. The spectacle is of a spineless regime content to recline on anti-Pakistan rhetoric while failing to protect its own citizens. India's evident intimidation by Pakistani nuclear sabre-rattling only reinforces the impression that New Delhi does not grasp the essentials of safeguarding national interests. Instead, it seems content to expand the US role as "facilitator" on all outstanding issues with Pakistan – a task for which our own National Security Adviser, Brajesh Mishra, increasingly appears to answer more to Washington than to the Indian public, implementing "Uncle Sam's" script in letter and spirit.

The core question is not whether we should engage Pakistan in dialogue - sooner or later we must - but whether, by repeatedly involving the US, we are undermining the Shimla Accord, which should remain the sole basis for any future bilateral negotiations. Given the changing political landscape across the border - notably the rise of the pro-Taliban MMA in recent elections - India should be tightening its vigil and preparing, if necessary, for pre-emptive strikes against terror infrastructure in Pakistan-occupied Kashmir. MMA-led governments in the NWFP and Balochistan pose a direct threat to Indian interests in Kashmir, since these religious parties can use state machinery to move Al-Qaeda elements now lying low into Jammu and Kashmir to escalate violence.

Despite intense US pressure, Pakistan has shown no real inclination to rein in militants operating under its intelligence wing and carrying out massacres of Hindus and relentless attacks on Indian security forces. Under these circumstances, New Delhi must begin working to isolate Islamabad internationally. The recent revelations of Pakistani nuclear assistance to Pyongyang, in blatant violation of non-proliferation norms, should make it easier for India to persuade the world that, despite its convenient alignment with Washington in the "war on terror", Pakistan remains insincere about its commitments and continues to function as the epicentre of a terror campaign across South Asia.

6.5 NEW DELHI AND ISLAMABAD: THE END GAME

January 2003

Kashmir has, time and again, been portrayed in the Western media as the 'nuclear flashpoint' between India and Pakistan in South Asia, and the international community has largely shared that view. In the post-13/12 crisis, amid heightened tensions, Western media went into overdrive, painting a picture of nuclear holocaust should India launch pre-emptive strikes against terrorist infrastructure across the Line of Control.

This campaign - you will pardon me for saying so - was aimed squarely at putting India on the back foot and, coupled with travel advisories issued by Western and 'friendly' governments, had a direct bearing on the prospects of either limited or full-scale war. One could even argue that this Western offensive, with tacit media support, emboldened Pakistan to stoop to nuclear blackmail against New Delhi. The rest is history.

New Delhi, for its part, has failed to capitalise on several opportunities, in large measure because US interests in protecting its client state, Pakistan, have consistently prevailed. India should have adopted a far harder line in exposing Pakistan's clandestine transfer of nuclear know-how to North Korea in exchange for missile technology. One can understand why Washington, which has known about these transactions all along, prefers to keep things under wraps, at least for now. What is harder to fathom is why India does not expose this nexus and share the information with the world. Please do not tell me the US is arm-twisting New Delhi into silence; that simply will not wash. The Indian leadership needs to explore alternative mechanisms of pressure on Pakistan, not limited to Washington alone.

General Pervez Musharraf's much-publicised 12 January speech was, as many have observed, a damp squib - nothing but a pack of lies aimed at appeasing the West and buying time. Our apprehensions have since been vindicated: first, Hafiz Saeed, chief of Lashkar-e-Taiba, and more recently Masood Azhar, chief of Jaish-e-Mohammad, have been freed. Not that there were ever meaningful restrictions on these organisations, even after Islamabad formally banned them following the Parliament attack. For these battle-hardened, well-armed Islamist militants, jihad in Kashmir is part of a worldwide religious crusade, not an effort to secure Kashmiris' right to self-determination, and they continue to enjoy ISI support through and through. Contrary to what Musharraf led us to believe, state sponsorship of these ultra-fundamentalist outfits was never truly withdrawn - no wonder they remain as lethal and ugly as ever.

Cross-border terrorism has two aspects: actual infiltration across the borders and the terrorist infrastructure that sustains it. Infiltration levels fluctuate over time along the Line of Control and the international border, but to treat that as proof that Pakistan has dealt firmly with terror groups would be simplistic and naïve. Islamabad can dial infiltration up or down at will, depending on circumstances; it must never be used as a yardstick to judge Pakistan's sincerity. The real test lies in the latter aspect: the camps themselves. The ground reality is that Pakistan has not dismantled these camps, US pressure notwithstanding. It may have relocated a few here and there, but that is the extent of it. To expect New Delhi to reciprocate while Pakistan has taken no meaningful steps to dismantle terror camps or end state sponsorship would be unrealistic. The ISI and large sections of the armed forces continue to patronise ultra-fundamentalist groups; Islamabad has merely been treating symptoms, leaving the disease - the terrorist infrastructure - untouched.

New Delhi has merit in arguing for dialogue with Valley separatists separately from any talks with Pakistan. In this endeavour, the PDP-led coalition has lent able support through its 'healing touch' policy. The tripartite talks demanded by the Hurriyat Conference - itself deeply divided on goals, means, and strategies, including whether to continue armed struggle or participate in electoral politics - do not hold merit and probably reflect Islamabad's bidding. As Delhi recognises, terrorism in Kashmir has domestic as well as Pakistani roots, making it all the more crucial that the state government's present approach succeeds.

We must reach out to the Kashmiri masses, and, as the chief minister rightly notes, first set our own house in order before tackling the larger issue. Yet let us harbour no illusions: Islamabad will do its utmost to scuttle this holistic initiative. Pakistan is the epitome of hypocrisy; to expect it not to deploy its 'territorial army' of jihadis to foment future trouble would be to ignore the obvious. This defunct democracy dared to dismiss Kashmir's October elections as a farce, even while blind to its own sham that installed Musharraf's puppet, Jamali, as prime minister.

As for talks with Islamabad, they must begin sooner or later. But for negotiations to move forward, sincerity and clarity of purpose are paramount - qualities Islamabad conspicuously lacks. If the stiff-upper-lip attitude of its establishment is any guide, the very rationale of sitting at the negotiating table is undermined. New Delhi's current stance stems from the belief that India can tolerate present levels of tension and violence, provided they do not escalate, and can meanwhile work out a settlement with Srinagar's leadership.

Islamabad appears to think it can piggyback on Washington to strong-arm New Delhi on Kashmir - a notion beyond the realm of realism in the post-9/11 era. Washington cannot be seen to support a regime that uses state-sponsored terrorism as an instrument of policy. The US is preoccupied with

Iraq, North Korea and even Iran; both it and the wider international community have little appetite for redrawing borders and may well favour converting the Line of Control into an international frontier - an option unacceptable to Pakistan's ruling elites.

Moreover, the US has learnt harsh lessons: 50 years of diplomacy, whether through the UN or unilateral channels, have produced no progress towards resolving the Kashmir dispute. US policymakers now realise that the burden lies with India and Pakistan, who know each other best, and that a good start is possible if both show a little more flexibility. Washington has wisely confined itself to the role of initiator and facilitator.

Islamabad's obsession with annexing Kashmir by hook or crook must eventually be abandoned. The sooner it recognises that continued support for insurgents is a dead-end option, the better for peace and prosperity in South Asia. The Pakistani military establishment and, more critically, the ISI that does the covert dirty work, must sooner or later accept that violence will never bring international intervention on terms favourable to Pakistan - indeed, the opposite is more likely. The problem is that Pakistan's policymakers do not want to normalise relations until Kashmir is resolved, and worse, the country has no domestic constituency pushing for rapprochement. To expect Islamabad under the present circumstances to alter ground realities in ways that make solutions possible does not seem realistic, though such a shift would certainly be a welcome change.

6.6 THE KASHMIR COMMITTEE: RAM IN THE US

January 2003

The Kashmir Committee, led by Ram Jethmalani, former Union Law Minister, which has been spearheading efforts to untangle the dreadlocks of the larger Kashmir issue, has taken one step forward and two backwards and is no closer to breaking the ice with separatists led by the All Parties Hurriyat Conference. The combative approach adopted by some Hurriyat Conference constituents has, in fact, raised serious doubts about the success of this initiative, which is largely a private-citizen effort, though it is known to have the blessing of one faction (read North Block) within the BJP-led coalition in New Delhi.

One of the KC's initial setbacks was its failure to bring separatist Kashmiri leaders into the October 2002 elections, despite tall promises by Ram Jethmalani to L. K. Advani himself. Once the separatist bandwagon began attaching strings, including a raft of preconditions, New Delhi developed cold feet and backtracked, leaving the KC high and dry. That has not deterred Jethmalani from pushing ahead in the post-election period.

Ground realities have, in fact, shifted significantly since the successful elections. The Hurriyat Conference and company - to borrow my own phrase, 'participate or perish' - have taken a serious image beating and, believe it or not, even the Americans, who had lent them a sympathetic ear, have begun distancing themselves after their own assessments. Robert Blackwill, US ambassador to India, on a recent trip to Jammu and Kashmir, was accorded a red-carpet welcome and met a wide cross-section of people - except for the Hurriyat Conference, which he pointedly disregarded.

To advance the KC agenda, Ram Jethmalani recently visited the US to lay the groundwork for Track-II diplomacy with Islamabad. Speaking at a Washington event - transcripts of which The Kashmir Telegraph has obtained - he heaped praise on General Pervez Musharraf, giving him a clean chit by stating that 'the only way to bring about this change [abandoning the hard-line stance] is through Musharraf. If he is replaced, things in Pakistan will deteriorate, with grave implications for the security of the world and of India.'

Jethmalani's endorsement of Musharraf is not altogether surprising, given that the parallel Kashmir Committee in Pakistan was itself set up by the General and is, unlike the Indian body, a largely official initiative. Despite continuous efforts, Jethmalani has been unable to arrange a meeting with his Pakistani counterparts because of heightened tensions, which hit a new low when New Delhi refused to attend the SAARC conference in Islamabad, forcing indefinite postponement. A more conciliatory tone towards Musharraf makes tactical sense if Jethmalani hopes he can broker a meeting between the two committees and thereby kickstart Track-II talks in which he himself wants a seat.

To that end, he even outlined the KC's blueprint, which calls, among other things, for a unilateral ceasefire by the Government of India against militant operations in Jammu and Kashmir. It bears recalling that Prime Minister Atal Bihari Vajpayee burnt his fingers during the Ramzan ceasefire of 2000; one-sided gestures designed to facilitate dialogue ironically tend to increase violence, since terrorist groups have more than a passing interest in strengthening their bargaining position before committing to talks. Moreover, radical Pakistan-based outfits such as Jamaat-ul-Mujahideen and Lashkar-e-Taiba have already shown a lackadaisical attitude towards any dialogue. They even issued a warning to Umar Farooq, the former Hurriyat Conference chairman, for inviting Jethmalani - a 'non-believer' - to an Iftaar party. The KC is understood to be in a catch-22, with New Delhi still non-committal, a situation widely seen as a setback to KC-sponsored Track-II diplomacy.

The KC blueprint also calls for 'the termination of all pending cases based on unjust accusations, after review by a small panel of judges; the release of all those wrongfully detained and of those whose detention serves no immediate security purpose; and a general amnesty for those who publicly forswear violence.' These assertions, though long known, have raised eyebrows in intelligence circles. While North Block has shown little interest, the PDP-led government has come to the KC's rescue by facilitating the release of some prominent erstwhile militant commanders.

Jethmalani, aware of the US capacity to arm-twist both Islamabad and New Delhi, was mild in criticising US foreign policy during his trip and instead trained his fire on New Delhi, which he believes has been scuttling his efforts to launch much-awaited Track-II talks. Emboldened by Prime Minister Vajpayee's earlier acknowledgement that mistakes were made in Kashmir, he went a step further in castigating the Government of India for having 'committed sins in Kashmir.'

Sandwiched between two extremist positions - secession on one side and reducing Jammu and Kashmir to a regular state on the other - Jethmalani has, credible sources confirm, taken a fancy to the Kathwari Plan and the recommendations of the Kashmir Study Group, proposals now understood to be under active consideration by the KC. The Study Group, incidentally, is considered close to the US administration, though it no longer wields the influence it did under Bill Clinton.

The initial run of setbacks suffered by the KC has much to do with Jethmalani's over-optimistic claims and an excess of public statements - something a negotiator should avoid at all costs, lest an atmosphere of suspicion develop when his pronouncements are conveniently twisted by those who wish to derail the peace process. By most accounts, the KC has enjoyed considerable goodwill; many in the Valley believe its heart is in the right place. But can it deliver the goods amid heightened tensions? An honest answer casts serious doubt on the entire initiative.

Last but not least, conspiracy theories doing the rounds in Delhi suggest that A. S. Dulat, senior officer, former RAW chief and now officer on special duty for Kashmir in the PMO, has a score to settle with the KC for having scuttled some of his covert initiatives and is fast regaining lost ground. No doubt Jethmalani is bewildered by the change of heart from his erstwhile benefactors in North Block. Abandoned by his own patrons and on a collision course with the PMO, he had little choice but to turn to Washington for help in salvaging his pet project.

6.7 HEY RAM: BIG EGO, SMALL MAN

January 2003

Ram Jethmalani, former Union Law Minister, has stooped to new lows - not that the occurrence is altogether surprising - to make his presence felt. Time and again, shamelessly, he defends General Pervez Musharraf in articles published in a particular newspaper, so we no longer need to turn to Dawn to read about the intrinsic merits of Musharraf and his junta regime. That Musharraf persists with his nuclear blackmail doctrine against India does not seem to matter to people like Jethmalani, who will continue to shower praise on him and make a hero out of him one way or the other.

To further his own personal agenda, Jethmalani has now taken on the task of defending one of the prime accused in the attack on the Indian Parliament, S. A..R. Geelani. Incidentally, Jethmalani was elected to the upper house of Parliament by Shiv Sena, and the party is now asking him to resign first and then shed tears for traitors and enemies. So much for these 'turncoat walas' who, in the name of justice, engage in acts that would put even genuine turncoats to shame. He has joined an elite league alongside the likes of P. Chidambaram, who, for huge sums of money, actually defended the defunct Dhabol Power Corporation, a subsidiary of Enron - a company that has set examples in corruption and malpractice, an epitome against which comparisons will long be made. Yet Chidambaram still thinks we should believe the half-intelligent commentary that arrives at our doorsteps on Sunday mornings, courtesy of an Indian newspaper.

Ram Jethmalani is known for his maverick behaviour and has in the past defended smuggler Haji Mastan and Kehar Singh in the Gandhi assassination case. India is not only fighting Pakistan in what is a legitimate battle against cross-border terrorism, but also the likes of Ram Jethmalani, who pose an equally dangerous internal threat and need to be taken to task for their newfound love of acting as defence counsel for General Musharraf and, more recently, the prime accused in the attack on Parliament. As far as the latter decision is concerned, Jethmalani has decided to don his black coat again with the singular rationale of breaking the ice with separatists - the Hurriyat Conference in particular and the pro-secession bandwagon in Kashmir in general. This, he feels, will earn him the much-needed brownie points to further the mission of his Kashmir Committee, which seems to have encountered roadblocks and is on the verge of being wound up.

Jethmalani is believed to be presently on a trip to Europe, and we sincerely hope that the tour is private and that he will not engage in the loose talk he indulged in when he was in Washington some time back, going on and on about how Musharraf was important for the peace and prosperity of the subcontinent. And we still talk about external threats to India!

The threat is very much internal, and such internal threats must be taken seriously. Individuals who champion the cause of a US client state, Pakistan, on the one hand, and lecturer-turned-terrorists who have waged war against India through despicable terrorist acts on the other, need to be shown their real worth - the sooner, the better.

And let us put a stop to the farce called the Kashmir Committee. Is somebody at South Block and North Block listening?

6.8 HURRIYAT HAS NO OPTION BUT TO INITIATE TALKS

February 2003

The All Parties Hurriyat Conference, known as Kul Jamaat Hurriyat Conference in the local lingo and better known by its acronym, Hurriyat Conference, is often portrayed as the 'political face' of the separatist bandwagon in Kashmir, with national and international media alike tending to exaggerate the significance of the conglomerate in the given scheme of things.

Though Hurriyat Conference is said to be an umbrella organisation of more than two dozen groups, the reality is that some of its constituents are so small that their existence in Kashmir's political spectrum is, by and large, inconsequential. To say that Hurriyat Conference consists primarily of about eight to ten significant groups would be to state the obvious.

Even some of the larger, better-known constituents, such as the Lone clan's People's Conference, have a limited sphere of influence confined to specific pockets in the Valley. Out of a dozen or so seats contested by proxy candidates in the October 2002 elections, the People's Conference managed to win only a solitary seat, though it must be said that it lost two other seats to the National Conference in close contests.

Most Hurriyat Conference members are separatists who favour an independent state, though some favour accession to Pakistan; one constituent, the Kashmir Bar Association, is apolitical in nature. Hurriyat Conference as an organisation is widely believed to be 'deeply divided on goals, means and strategies, including whether to continue the armed struggle or participate in the political process.'

In the post-election scenario, Hurriyat Conference is fast

losing hope and, if a statement by its executive council member M. A. Ansari is any indication, the conglomerate has climbed down from its long-standing position - insistence on tripartite talks involving India, Pakistan and the people of Kashmir (read Hurriyat Conference). Instead, it has agreed in principle to hold direct, one-to-one negotiations with New Delhi's designated representative.

Having failed to participate in the elections, largely because 'most Hurriyat Conference leaders have only a narrow individual following and no real political experience', it is now vital for the organisation to bring itself back into reckoning - a do-or-die situation - by opening negotiations with New Delhi.

Commenting on these developments, a Home Ministry official, speaking on condition of anonymity, told Kashmir Telegraph that they represent 'a way forward' and are being 'carefully monitored'. Other sources confirm, however, that New Delhi will not rush the process and will take its time deciding on future steps, only after gauging reactions from Islamabad.

Kashmir policymakers within government see these developments as vindication of New Delhi's position, which calls for talks with separatist elements in the Valley independently of any dialogue with Pakistan. Despite Hurriyat Conference insistence that Pakistan be accommodated at some later stage, officials described the climb-down as a 'major policy shift' within the separatist camp.

Many believe the dialogue process will be welcomed by Kashmiris. Initial reactions suggest the Hurriyat Conference is also keen, prompted by the fact that it is rapidly losing credibility and influence while the PDP is the major beneficiary. The development is also seen in politico-diplomatic circles as a serious setback to the Ram Jethmalani-led Kashmir Committee, which has been accused of double-talk by some important Hurriyat Conference constituents.

Political observers in the Valley attach great significance to the start of talks, pointing out that otherwise the Hurriyat Conference risks being reduced to playing second fiddle to the PDP, which has been making rapid inroads into areas where the Hurriyat Conference's writ has been supreme since the onset of militancy over a decade ago.

One of the Hurriyat Conference's stated positions over time has been that violence and gun culture cannot serve as the means of achieving what it describes as the right to self-determination for the people of Kashmir (though some constituents dispute this stand). Sooner or later, therefore, it must come to the negotiating table.

Speaking on condition of anonymity, a high-ranking Hurriyat Conference member told Kashmir Telegraph from New Delhi that there is a consensus within the party ranks on the urgent need to start negotiations with the Indian leadership as soon as possible. 'We cannot wait for normalisation of relations between India and Pakistan, which, if indications are to be believed, have hit a new low rather than improving. Under the circumstances, we have little option but to get on with the negotiation process,' the official said, explaining the party's position.

One major setback for the Hurriyat Conference has been the volte-face by the US State Department, whose senior officials used to meet Hurriyat Conference delegations on visits to New Delhi, providing a measure of patronage. With no Christina Rocca-type figures to lend a sympathetic ear, the Hurriyat Conference is finding it increasingly difficult to advance an agenda that has, to a large extent, been dictated by stern instructions from the Pakistani embassy in New Delhi. Indications are, however, that the party is now set to pursue its own agenda, which calls for talks with New Delhi without Pakistani involvement, at least to begin with.

Pakistan and militant groups with foreign mercenaries in their ranks have been marginalised by the successful Kashmir elections. Neither will welcome a dialogue process between the Hurriyat Conference and New Delhi, and both will be tempted to play the spoiler. That some senior Hurriyat Conference figures have in the past been bullied by militant organisations at Islamabad's behest is well known, with the result that the party has often blindly toed the Pakistani line.

However, with Kashmiris increasingly disillusioned by the Hurriyat Conference's stance, the party has little choice but to open talks with New Delhi, even at the risk of personal danger to its leaders. Though the political situation in Kashmir remains fragile to some extent, the 'peace constituency', which had been passive for some time, has now become active.

6.9 VOHRA IN, JETHMALANI OUT

March 2003

New Delhi has eventually appointed the long-awaited interlocutor to commence parleys with both the elected representatives of the Jammu and Kashmir state legislative assembly and the separatist bandwagon, including the All Parties Hurriyat Conference (Hurriyat Conference). N. N. Vohra, former Home Secretary, is the Centre's choice. Other names initially doing the rounds were K. C. Pant, former negotiator; A. S. Dulat, former chief of the Research and Analysis Wing (RAW); Wajahat Habibullah; and Union Law Minister Arun Jaitley.

There was also considerable speculation that New Delhi might appoint two separate interlocutors: one for talks with elected representatives already part of the national mainstream, the other for separatists representing other shades of public opinion. Some think-tanks within government were of the view that holding negotiations with separatists separately from parleys with the elected legislature would, in the long run, prove beneficial.

Arun Jaitley was tipped as chief negotiator for talks with elected representatives, given his expertise in legal and constitutional matters. It is reliably learnt, however, that senior BJP leaders were averse to the party directly involving itself in the peace process, fearing the complexity of the subject could put the party in a spot of bother with Sangh Parivar outfits, especially the Vishwa Hindu Parishad, central to the party's hopes in forthcoming state assembly elections.

In the first place, the BJP was not particularly keen on launching the peace process at this stage and wanted more time to increase pressure on the separatist bandwagon and further weaken their position before holding talks. On the other hand, given Prime Minister Atal Bihari Vajpayee's own promise from the ramparts of the Red Fort during his Independence Day speech to hold dialogue, the BJP had little choice but to give in to Chief Minister Mufti Sayeed's insistence and appoint N. N. Vohra.

A seasoned bureaucrat, 66-year-old Vohra has served as Principal Secretary to former Prime Minister I. K. Gujral and, as Defence Secretary, headed a committee that investigated the politician–criminal nexus in 1995. A fine administrator, Vohra dealt with the Kashmir problem in his capacity as Home Secretary and is no stranger to the convolutions of the Kashmir issue. He later chaired the committee on internal security set up following the Subramaniam Committee report on the conditions that led to the Kargil war, and has been a firm advocate of 'stringent laws to meet the challenge posed by rising militancy.' Speaking at a seminar in January 2000, Vohra argued that TADA had failed to address the situation effectively and that those who speak of human rights should assess the ground reality in Jammu & Kashmir, where terrorists have killed thousands, 'and our existing legal system has failed to combat terrorism there.'

The PDP-led coalition has welcomed the fresh initiative, with Chief Minister Mufti Sayeed describing the developments as 'very good news'. It is pertinent to recall that the Common Minimum Programme (CMP) of the PDP-Congress alliance stipulated that the state government would request the Government of India to initiate and hold wide-ranging consultations and dialogue, without preconditions, with elected representatives and other sections to evolve a 'broad-based consensus on restoration of peace.' This fresh initiative gives new life to the PDP, whose domestic constituency in Kashmir had begun to feel disillusioned by the party's failure to persuade New Delhi to commence talks.

The focus now shifts to what, in diplomatic parlance, is called the 'brief' or 'terms of reference' for the proposed talks, which will be set by New Delhi - more specifically, North Block - for its new interlocutor before negotiations officially begin. One reason K. C. Pant, former interlocutor on Kashmir, failed to break the ice with separatists was that his 'brief was limited', leaving him little room to take the initiative to any logical conclusion.

Hurriyat Conference, one of the main separatist groups with which Vohra is likely to hold discussions, has been, as expected, guarded in its response - though it is reliably learnt that the body has agreed in principle to start negotiations with the designated interlocutor. The initial official Hurriyat Conference reaction available to the author states that the amalgam hopes a dialogue process will be set in motion to find a 'permanent and lasting solution' to the Kashmir issue in line with the wishes of the people, the party's official position, except that there is no mention of Islamabad's involvement, a definite climb-down.

It is worth noting that Hurriyat Conference, Pakistan Chapter, has termed the appointment of a fresh negotiator by New Delhi a futile exercise, insisting that fruitful negotiations on Kashmir require the involvement of all three parties: New Delhi, Islamabad and the people of Kashmir - typical Pakistani parrot-speak.

Past peace initiatives on Kashmir have not yielded the desired results, which prompts one to view this fresh initiative with an element of scepticism. One wonders what happened to earlier interlocutors like K. C. Pant, Arun Jaitley and Ram Jethmalani. Did they achieve any measure of success in unshackling the dreadlocks of the larger Kashmir issue? If so, why has the government not officially disclosed the outcome of these past initiatives?

The people of India also deserve to know the 'terms of reference' or 'brief' for the proposed talks. Enough of this farce in the name of Kashmir. We must have one coherent policy on Kashmir. Is somebody at North Block listening?

6.10 TIME TO GO THAT EXTRA MILE IN KASHMIR

May 2003

Prime Minister Atal Bihari Vajpayee has undoubtedly made history. He has the distinction of being the first Indian premier in 17 years to address a 'well-attended' public gathering in the heart of Srinagar in Kashmir. Let us please forget how successful, well-attended political rallies are managed; the mechanism is the same, whether organised in Srinagar or Patna, or for that matter, Lahore or Karachi.

Symbolism apart, Vajpayee has indeed earned, if nothing else, a few brownie points - a blend of poet-politician at his very best. On the first leg - Day 1 of his much-publicised visit, when he interfaced with the people of Kashmir - he chose, conveniently, to put aside all contentious issues, displaying his charisma and poetic acumen. Striking a conciliatory note, Vajpayee talked and talked about peace - the need for peace. And of course, he surprised many when he extended a hand of friendship to Pakistan. He only chose to raise thorny issues on Day 2 of his historic visit.

Talk of reactions and you had Islamabad in a spot of bother, at least to begin with. Taken altogether by surprise at Vajpayee's peace offer, Pakistan recovered in time to welcome the initiative and, once again, remarked upon the statesman-like qualities of Vajpayee. However, if his Day 1 musings were for the peace constituency in Jammu & Kashmir, his parting shot just before flying back to Delhi was aimed squarely at his own domestic constituency in the rest of the country - and, of course, at section(s) of his own government.

At the end of Day 1, the hawkish elements must have been in such a frenzy at the turn of events that External Affairs Minister Yashwant Sinha must have found it difficult to find a hiding place - or perhaps thought he should try to prevent Vajpayee's flight from landing in Delhi as a mark of protest for being made to look like a fool. At the end of his two-day visit, the prime minister reminded us that, no, he did not forget to mention - say - the Nadimarg massacre, where 24 Hindu civilians were killed by militants, but simply chose not to, because he wanted to make a new beginning. By the end of his journey, he was again his usual self, reiterating India's known position on the prerequisites to be met by Pakistan for any meaningful dialogue on Kashmir.

Talk of making new beginnings, and Vajpayee will be attempting it for the third time - that is, if we live to see the day. At least our dear premier is giving it another sincere try; the least we, the loyal countrymen, can do is look the other way and hope that there is not another war debacle or, for that matter, another terror attack on our Parliament. Third time lucky for talks with Pakistan - we hope so. At least there is a positive start, with the premier announcing the restoration of full diplomatic ties and air links. On the first leg of his journey, he perhaps gave enough leeway to Islamabad to make the best of his conciliatory gestures.

Pakistan, it seems, was so moved by Vajpayee's statesmanship that President General Pervez Musharraf's poster-boy, Prime Minister Zafar Ullah Khan Jamali, coolly picked up the phone and spoke to Vajpayee for about ten minutes. Apart from exchanging pleasantries, they appear to have got down to discussing, among other things, 'relevant issues.' Washington, London, Paris, Beijing - everyone was thrilled, happy. Peace has been given a chance in South Asia; nuclear holocaust has been averted. So far, so good.

What next? First, let us not go on a warmongering spree and be the spoilsports by refusing to give peace a chance. Fast forward. It would seem really odd that, while Jamali is playing perfect host to Vajpayee, treating him to tasty desserts, our poor Havaldar Shinde continues to fight a grim battle for survival. Havaldar Shinde, let me explain, is with the Rashtriya Rifles, posted in the Doda–Rajouri sector, engaged in counter-insurgency operations. Dutifully, against all odds, he smokes out bigwigs of militant groups, smashing their hideouts in the deep, thick jungle of Doda.

He, too, deserves peace – if not a good meal – at a time when his prime minister is talking peace. He could make use of this peace to muster the courage to write a postcard, if not an email, to his commanding officer about his experiences in counter-insurgency operations: his impressions, what he needs in terms of logistics and equipment to make his operations even more successful.

India and Pakistan should talk; no one in their right mind would dispute such a need. But it is also imperative that peace be given a chance in Kashmir – in the true sense, in a way that bloodshed stops, at least temporarily. That has to be done, the sooner the better. The least Pakistan can do at this crucial juncture is impress upon the United Jihad Council – the conglomerate of all terrorist outfits operating in Jammu and Kashmir – to call, say, a two-month moratorium on its violent activities. Pakistan can bring this about discreetly. It is not a tough request; it is a very reasonable, sensible way to create an atmosphere of utmost good faith – one of the essential ingredients for healthy, meaningful discussion.

6.11 DATELINE KASHMIR: THE PARTITION PLAN

July 2003

The purpose of this article is not to focus on what to do tomorrow. It focuses on what to do today - perhaps accept that our rejection of the two-nation theory was rubbished to the historical dustbin long ago - 14 years, to be precise - by an important ingredient of our own pluralistic society; in contemplation - possible give-and-take on Kashmir - of tomorrow.

That the Kashmiri separatist bandwagon, spearheaded by the All Parties Hurriyat Conference (Hurriyat Conference), is leaving no stone unturned in impressing upon the United States (hereafter referred to as You-Know-Who, to borrow a Harry Potterism) to 'force' New Delhi to make 'concessions' on Kashmir clearly indicates its extreme anxiety at being unable to make much headway with the objectives of its so-called 'movement' for what it describes as the right to self-determination of the people of Kashmir. Post-October 2002 elections in Jammu and Kashmir, Hurriyat Conference seems finally to have realised that the only viable way, perhaps, to revive its sagging fortunes would be to petition the most powerful nation - You-Know-Who - for help.

There exists a 'very powerful' - pro-Musharraf - Kashmiri lobby in Washington that has been 'furiously lobbying the Bush White House to 'turn the screws' on Vajpayee to give a role in the Jammu and Kashmir administration to pro-jihadi elements close to Hurriyat Conference.' And the 'Chenab Plan' - brainchild of the Kashmir Study Group headed by Farooq Kathwari - is, it is reliably learnt, 'being backed in private talks by the (You-Know-Who) State Department, which has even designated a 'well-regarded' officer as its 'Kashmir officer'.'

It is astounding that American Kashmiris have been able to pass off terrorism in Kashmir as some kind of a freedom struggle. What is more intriguing is that You-Know-Who - the so-called leader of the global war on terror - perhaps seems to be buying the argument. Kashmiri American Ghulam Nabi Fai, who has been actively raising funds and sending money to Kashmir to fuel militancy, of the Kashmiri American Council has well-established Pakistani links and is associated with the fundamentalist Jamaat-e-Islami. He has been advocating a role for separatist Kashmiri leadership in any future dialogue between India and Pakistan.

Fai is being mentioned in both political and diplomatic circles, in New Delhi and Washington, with alarming frequency for his extremely proactive role and is known to have garnered tacit support from various influential Senators, Congressmen, lobbyists and, of course, two very influential think-tanks - the Centre for Strategic and International Studies and the Stimson Centre, to name a few - for his sinister plans to bring about partition of Jammu and Kashmir on communal lines.

In the last week of May this year, a high-level delegation of the You-Know-Who embassy in New Delhi, comprising Political Counsellor Matthew G. Boyse and Secretary for Political Affairs William P. Hurd, met JKLF leader Yasin Malik for over an hour. The specifics of what transpired are not exactly known, but it is reliably learnt that the discussion revolved widely around the particulars of the 'Chenab Plan'. That this was more than a routine meeting assumes significance from the fact that, straight after this not-so-secret meeting, JKLF embarked on a signature campaign to ascertain the wishes of the people of Kashmir. Is there a connection?

Overall, emboldened by an overwhelming response from You-Know-Who, Hurriyat Conference has meanwhile decided to open branches in the United States and some European countries, the Middle East and the Far East. It is reliably learnt that moves are afoot to rope in prominent non-resident Kashmiri leaders actively working for the Kashmir cause to head offices in New York, London, Toronto, Brussels, Kuala Lumpur, Jeddah and elsewhere.

Did I hear you ask where the ideologue of the militant outfit Hizb-ul-Mujahideen, Syed Ali Shah Geelani, is these days? Well, he is certainly not hiding. Geelani has simply been asked by friends of You-Know-Who to lie low for a while. He has no role whatsoever to play at this stage. Stage I of the act – to arm-twist a BJP-led India into making maximum concessions on Kashmir – is strictly for those who qualify as peaceniks in the so-called 'movement'. Only after Stage I is a resounding success – Muslim-majority areas of Jammu and Kashmir are accorded a quasi-sovereign status – are the services of the likes of Geelani likely to be pressed into action.

Building on the success of Stage I, the role of hawkish elements like Geelani would involve capitalising on the gains to launch a radical programme that would pave the way for the integration – yes – of Kashmir with Pakistan. Amen! After all, the integration of a 'semi-independent' Kashmir with Pakistan should be a cakewalk. There you see Mr Geelani all smiles. Need I say more?

That these hectic behind-the-scenes parleys may finally have paid dividends became evident on 13 June 2003, when India's Deputy Prime Minister, L. K. Advani, in a lecture delivered at Chicago, said that India was ready for a 'compromise' on Jammu and Kashmir. His give-and-take talk to achieve peace must surely have brought 1,000-watt smiles to the faces of Hurriyat Conference and company – and, more importantly, the You-Know-Who administration, which, it seems, played an important role in impressing upon him the need to give a little more leeway to Pakistan on Kashmir so that Islamabad can tone down the jihadi elements. How else can one explain the placatory sound-bites of Advani, who is known for his hard-line gospel on Kashmir and has, time and again, advocated the abrogation of Article 370, which gives special status to the only Muslim-majority Indian state?

His conciliatory pep talk has made peaceniks very happy indeed. Not to be left behind, even the warmongers are feeling 'glad'. President Musharraf, in his own words, is 'very glad that he (Advani) is prepared to make 'compromises' on Kashmir.' In the whole episode, it is not difficult to comprehend the 'give part' as far as India is concerned - that is easy. But what is India going to get in return? Probably peace of mind? Will the Man of Iron, L. K. Advani - mind you, even iron rusts - please care to explain the 'take part' to the people of this country?

The groundwork for adopting a more conciliatory approach - in line with the wishes of You-Know-Who - was set rolling as early as March this year, when Advani hinted at some kind of a compromise deal. He said - while referring to N. N. Vohra's brief - that he (Vohra) would, among other things, 'explore the option of devolution of greater powers to the state (Jammu and Kashmir). "Now, purely from the BJP's point of view, why should you do that, if the 'principles' you claim to stand by mean anything to you? After all, abrogation of the controversial Article 370 is very much on its agenda (at least that is what we are given to understand and led to believe). You cannot do away with Article 370 because of the compulsions of coalition politics - that is understandable. But why should the BJP undertake an exercise - devolve more powers to Jammu and Kashmir - that will make abrogation of Article 370 next to impossible, if the party is sincere about its past commitments?

There is more. Advani, in the same statement, noted that there was a strong case for devolution of more powers to the states, especially Jammu and Kashmir, which has a 'special history' that must be taken note of. Special history? What special history are we talking about? Even the Nawabs and Nizams - Advani loves Sardar Patel for cutting them to size - or, for that matter, the Scindias of Gwalior, have a 'special history'. So, what about them? His changed script - at the behest of You-Know-Who - not only belittles his own gospel but is also a sure-shot recipe for disaster that can only lead to the balkanisation of India. Just because Jammu and Kashmir is a Muslim-majority state does not mean it has a 'special history'.

The big problem both for Vajpayee and Advani is that they cannot undo the history of their own party, especially that of the BJP's predecessor, the Bharatiya Jana Sangh. Teaming up with Praja Parishad - in those days the Sangh's political front in Jammu and Kashmir - the BJS agitated against the special status of Jammu and Kashmir and paid a profound price in the death of Dr Syama Prasad Mookerjee, the party's founder-president, in Srinagar jail. He died under dubious circumstances, after being incarcerated for having led a batch of satyagrahis defying the ban on his entry into the state.

It seems - again, purely from the BJP's point of view - that they are willing to forget even the sacrifices of their own founder-president, 'Shyam Babu' as he was popularly called, for which I am sure they will earn no brownie points.

Meanwhile Musharraf is turning out to be a 'big pain in the ass' for the Indian establishment, especially the PMO. As I write, Musharraf has extracted a whopping five-year, $3 billion package from You-Know-Who, half of which goes for defence (George, are you listening?) matters, in return for Pakistan's cooperation in the global war on terror - this is what you call a win-win situation. But that is not the only cause of worry for New Delhi. It is his 'K' remark that is making India uneasy.

Musharraf has not only justified the Kargil war in the most

explicit way a head of state can, but even remains non-committal about another Kargil-like invasion in the near future. Not only that, he made the threat all the more explicit when he said that 'it's only when peace fails, violence occurs in 'any form'.' Any form, mind you! Interesting. (Seema Mustafa of the Asian Age will perhaps not agree with my interpretation, which has perhaps more to do with the fact that she is interacting far too often with Ram Jethmalani, President of the India Chapter of PML-QA.)

Talk of Kargil, and this sends our Prime Minister, Vajpayee, into a frenzy. He just cannot stand the 'K' word. Coming this time from the horse's mouth - Musharraf is considered the architect of the Kargil war - Vajpayee lost his cool and made those famous remarks that Pakistan is preparing for a 'fourth defeat'. Fourth defeat? I thought it should have been fifth, if one includes the Kargil war. Perhaps Vajpayee does not consider the outcome - pushing back of the Pakistani army onto the Line of Control - as a victory. How very enlightening! Thanks.

One of the problems for the Indian establishment has been its inability to 'define' the Kashmir issue. The specifics and dynamics of the vexed Kashmir issue are far deeper-rooted than the usual attempts to define concerns and controversies that are being passed off as realities. Kashmir - as an issue - is fundamentally a symbol of ideological dispute between India and Pakistan over the success or failure of the two-nation theory (that Muslims and Hindus cannot coexist), based on which Pakistan was established as a separate entity for the Muslims of undivided India.

The separation of East Pakistan and the creation of Bangladesh over 20 years ago demonstrated that, at times, regionalism can prevail over religious cohesiveness as a binding force. But India tends to overemphasise the significance of this more-than-20-year-old event - conveniently, perhaps - to justify the success mantra of her rejection of the two-nation theory, which served as the basis for the establishment of a pluralistic society and polity, with India ending up with more Muslims than Pakistan has (no offence meant).

So whose ideological theory - India's or Pakistan's - is right, and will prevail at the end of the day? The answer to this more-than-56-year-old question, unfortunately, lies in the resolution of the vexed Kashmir issue. Should Jammu and Kashmir - the only Muslim-majority state of the Indian Union - continue to remain with India, the Indian position is reinforced, ideologically speaking.

However, should it happen that Muslim-majority areas of Jammu and Kashmir accede to Pakistan or gain independence (theoretically, the degree of freedom is not of consequence), that is where things start to get tricky - very tricky - not only for the Indian establishment but for a very important component of our pluralistic society: the Indian Muslims. The scenario would mean that the underlying principle on which India was founded would hold no meaning and hence become null and void. What does that mean? It means that, after 56 years, India has come around to accept Pakistan's ideological stand that Muslims and Hindus cannot coexist.

However, the two-nation theory cannot - should not - be selectively applied (to Jammu and Kashmir). And that is where the most painful part comes into play. It would be unfortunate that, for the actions of the Kashmiri Muslims (here and hereafter, I am generalising for the sake of theoretical simplicity), Indian Muslims would end up paying a price. The price would be that they would lose the right to be part of Indian society. As such, should India lose Jammu and Kashmir because of the Muslim character of the state, Indian Muslims - in 1947 they had a choice whether to remain in India or Pakistan - would have no choice but to transport themselves to Pakistan.

In other words, to put it plainly, Pakistan would end up

getting what it wanted most all these years - Kashmir. But it does not come alone. Islamabad would also have to accept Muslims from other parts of India. What we are looking at is a second partition. That is what we are looking at, should India have to part ways with Kashmir, in any form? The future of Indian Muslims is very much - whether we like it or not - linked to how events unfold hereafter in Jammu and Kashmir; and, more importantly, the way Kashmiri Muslims conduct themselves will have a deep bearing on how Hindu-majority India looks at its Muslim brethren.

Are some half-forgotten lessons of the past becoming relevant again? The above scenario would mean many things (to interpret correctly, I lack both the authority and competence), but the most important would be that the unfinished business of Partition would finally be over. And India and Pakistan lived happily ever after?

PS: Kashmiri Muslims accepted, in principle, the two-nation theory in 1989-90, when, in a well-planned and executed pogrom, the minuscule Kashmiri Pandit minority - which lent pluralistic character to society and polity in Kashmir - was forced to flee the Valley and seek refuge in the 'Hindu-majority' parts of India. (JKLF, which these days poses as a peacenik, was instrumental in killing hundreds of KPs.)

Why has India chosen to remain silent over 'this' acceptance of the two-nation theory, which rubbishes the 'principles' and 'values' on which the Republic of India stands?

6.12 WHO WOULD BE NEW DELHI'S INTERLOCUTOR?

December 2003

It is as good as official. The 'Kashmir Committee' set up by Ram Jethmalani is on the verge of being wound up, after Jethmalani chose to step in as defence counsel for S. A. R. Geelani, one of the prime accused in the attack on the Indian Parliament, much against the advice of North Block, which had been providing a measure of patronage to the committee.

Jethmalani is also believed to have earned himself a bad name after he made disparaging remarks about the Home Ministry's suspension of the passport of former Hurriyat Conference chairman Mirwaiz Omar, shortly before he was due to embark on what was described as a 'private visit' abroad.

It is common knowledge that it was Deputy Prime Minister L. K. Advani himself who gave the green signal to Jethmalani to set up a private citizens' group consisting of eminent Indian intellectuals to seek out and break the ice with the separatist bandwagon in Kashmir, above all, the hard-to-pin-down All Parties Hurriyat Conference (Hurriyat Conference). That was, however, before the election process in Kashmir, when it was generally felt that the Hurriyat Conference's involvement, if not essential, was desirable for the overall health of the democratic process.

Nevertheless, the Kashmir Committee failed in its primary objective to rope in the Hurriyat Conference, something that did not go down well in New Delhi. Furthermore, in the post-election scenario, New Delhi's position on Kashmir has strengthened considerably, and any future negotiations with the Hurriyat Conference and company will take place largely on 'terms and conditions' laid down by the Home Ministry.

Hurriyat Conference, if indications are to be believed, is more likely to tone down its familiar rhetoric and get on with the task of negotiation, which it feels is the only way to reinforce its position within its own constituency in Kashmir - a base that, if emerging trends are any signal, is dwindling with each passing day.

The recent reshuffle of the Union Cabinet undertaken by the BJP offers a few pointers to the expected policy measures likely to be adopted by New Delhi vis-à-vis Kashmir. L. K. Advani's position has been considerably consolidated and, from now on, it is likely to be Advani's 'hardliner' policy all the way. A tough, antagonistic, hardline approach towards the separatist bandwagon is also in line with the desired position of the RSS (and other Sangh Parivar outfits), and many believe it is a 'crucial ingredient' for the party's rejuvenated 'nationalism' mantra in the forthcoming elections to nine states, including Himachal Pradesh and Madhya Pradesh, which are due soon.

Not to be left behind, MoS for Home I. D. Swami wrote an article for a leading national daily some time back, launching a scathing attack on Mirwaiz Omar and his brand of separatist politics, signalling the likely trends to emerge from New Delhi. Such hard-hitting articles - which have more to do with Omar's antagonistic position towards India in a BBC interview some time back, something that really annoyed the Home Ministry - are going to continue.

Nevertheless, it is also generally felt that New Delhi must undertake talks not only with the separatist leadership but also with the elected representatives of the state legislative assembly. The 'present timing' for the proposed talks has two primary reasons. First, it is better to engage separatists now, given that their position is considerably weakened, not only within their own constituency in Kashmir but also in the eyes of various influential think-tanks with considerable say in the policy decisions of various Western countries.

Second, and most important, the Hurriyat Conference has in principle agreed to hold negotiations without involving Islamabad, at least at this stage, in line with New Delhi's principled stand, which calls for talks with the Hurriyat Conference and company separately from any consultations with Islamabad on all outstanding issues, including Kashmir.

Furthermore, the PDP-led government in the state is also insisting that New Delhi should, as soon as possible, commence negotiations not only with members of the legislature but also with representatives who symbolise the 'other section of public opinion' (read Hurriyat Conference). The PDP has wisely chosen not to dwell on the 'nuts and bolts' of the larger Kashmir issue and has instead concentrated on good governance and, more importantly, economic revival of the troubled state.

There has, however, been mounting pressure from within its own constituency in Kashmir and, more importantly, from some separatist groups that provided clandestine support during the October 2002 elections, to take the lead in facilitating talks with New Delhi.

As a matter of fact, hectic behind-the-scenes parleys are currently underway, with intermediaries holding informal consultations with the separatist bandwagon, including Hurriyat Conference, to discuss the 'modalities and broader framework' of the proposed talks. New Delhi is also believed to be playing it 'extra safe' this time, given that its talks with Naga rebels remained inconclusive despite the flexibility shown by both sides.

For the position of New Delhi's 'chief interlocutor' for the proposed talks, three names are doing the rounds: Wajahat Habibullah, who successfully mediated the Hazratbal siege by militants in the 1990s; A. S. Dulat, senior officer and former head of RAW, now officer on special duty for Kashmir in the PMO; and K. C. Pant, Deputy Chairman of the Planning

Commission and a former mediator on Kashmir.

Amarjit Singh Dulat, who has all along been in touch with the separatist leadership, including the Hurriyat Conference, appeared to be the front-runner, given his vast experience as RAW chief. But Mufti Sayeed, it appears, is no longer comfortable with Dulat, which has prompted North Block and the PMO to explore other candidates. It is pertinent to recall that, until not long ago, Mufti Sayeed and Dulat shared an excellent rapport. However, the recent exclusion of a close confidant of Dulat, B. K. Vaishnavi (a PDP leader from the Kashmiri Pandit community), from the recently expanded Council of Ministers in Jammu and Kashmir has led to antagonistic feelings between the two, with Dulat explicitly making known his displeasure.

Chief Minister Mufti Sayeed is believed to favour K. C. Pant as the interlocutor for talks with both representatives and separatists. It may be recalled that Pant's first mission on Kashmir did not achieve much success, with the Hurriyat Conference then adopting an antagonistic approach, refusing to talk without Islamabad's participation. What his Mission Kashmir (Part I) did achieve was a vertical split in Hizbul Mujahideen, though that was largely attributed to Dulat and company.

But it is more than likely that Pant (who appears to be the front-runner) will be able to break the ice this time, with separatists more than eager to occupy positions across the negotiating table. To say that talks are inevitable would be to state the obvious. However, to expect the process to throw up clear-cut solutions to the complex Kashmir issue in the very near future would not be realistic. The negotiation process, when underway, is going to be prolonged, with the two sides sticking to their guns (read public posturing) to begin with. But, yes, it would be a beginning in the right direction.

CHAPTER 7: GLOBAL AND COMPARATIVE CONTEXT

The final chapter gathers four essays that step outside the immediate Jammu and Kashmir storyline but remain central to how I, as a strategic analyst, understood the wider security and geopolitical environment in which Kashmir sat. Together, they show that the dilemmas India faced in the Valley—about insurgency, delayed coercion, state capacity and great-power overreach—were part of a larger pattern, from the Himalayas to West Asia and even to our own forests.

In "Nepal: Red Flag Flying" (May 2002), I examine the Maoist insurgency next door and argue that it was never a purely Nepali domestic issue. The piece traces how decades of fragile monarchy, failed democratic experiments, and socio-economic neglect created fertile ground for a radical Left movement that drew ideological sustenance from abroad and tactical support from the porous Indo-Nepal border. I warn that if India treated Nepal's war as a distant problem, it would soon find the same networks intersecting with Naxalite groups at home, while China quietly positioned itself as a long-term beneficiary of a weakened Himalayan buffer. The core lesson is that counter-insurgency cannot be compartmentalised by map lines when the terrain, ideology and supply routes are shared.

"Is the US Going the USSR Way?" (January 2003) shifts the lens to Washington in the run-up to the Iraq war. Here I argue that the United States, intoxicated by its post-Cold War dominance, was beginning to mimic the very imperial overreach that broke the Soviet Union—stretching itself across multiple theatres, relying excessively on covert action and regime change, and underestimating the blowback from humiliating smaller states. I connect this critique back to South Asia by pointing out how American indulgence toward Pakistani dictators, driven by short-term needs in Afghanistan and the "war on terror", had shielded Islamabad from paying the full price for nurturing jihadist proxies. For me, this was not abstract anti-Americanism; it was a warning that great-power hubris was distorting the incentives of a state central to the Kashmir conflict.

In "A Tale of Two Fugitives" (January 2003), I juxtapose Veerappan and Osama bin Laden to make a point about delayed state action. The essay compares a sandalwood smuggler-bandit operating in India's forests and the world's most wanted terrorist hiding in the badlands of West Asia, and notes a common pattern: years of half-hearted pursuit, political interference, and even local romanticising created a form of Stockholm syndrome in the affected populations. I argue that when the state hesitates to apply "drastic surgery" to entrenched violent actors, it not only emboldens them but also corrodes public faith in institutions. The subtext for Kashmir is clear: a democracy cannot afford to normalise the presence of armed non-state power centres, whether they wear the mask of "rebels", "smugglers" or "freedom fighters".

"The Lost Valley" (July 2002) brings the focus back to Kashmir's landscape and people, but in a reflective, almost elegiac register. In that piece, I contrast the Valley's extraordinary natural beauty and the memories of an earlier, more open Kashmir with the socio-economic devastation wrought by years of militancy and misgovernance. I describe how the entire region—Valley, Jammu and Ladakh—has paid the price in lost tourism, broken infrastructure, disrupted administration and a pervasive sense of suspended normal life. The essay is less about policy prescriptions and more about reminding the reader what has been squandered: a place that could have been one of South Asia's great success stories, reduced, by violence and state failure on both sides of the Line of Control, to a metaphor for loss.

Taken together, these four essays explain why I have never seen Jammu and Kashmir as an isolated "local issue". Nepal's Maoist war showed how insurgencies travel across mountain borders; America's post-9/11 choices shaped Pakistan's room for manoeuvre; Veerappan's long run highlighted the dangers of living with festering threats; and "The Lost Valley" underlined the civilisational and economic stakes of conflict becoming a way of life. The chapter is therefore not a miscellaneous dump; it is the global and comparative context that frames the arguments made in the core Jammu and Kashmir chapters.

7.1 NEPAL: RED FLAG FLYING

May 2002

Clubbed between two Asian powers, India and China, Nepal has been undergoing the worst political upheaval in its history. The largely supported 'People's Movement' in 1990 paved the way for the establishment of a constitutional democratic system, but for the past six years, the Himalayan nation has been unable to contain Maoist insurgency. Media reports suggest that more than 4,500 people have lost their lives; Maoist attacks, police and army actions are the order of the day, and more than half the kingdom has been reeling under a spate of violent activities. There is growing evidence that Maoist activities appear extensive, with large armies of rebels attacking army and police posts. Commenting on the motivation and ideology, Chitra K. Tiwari, strategic analyst, says: 'The movement feeds on poverty, discontent with repressive policies, and corruption. The highly confrontational character of the country's mainstream politics has been a weak counterweight. The outlook is for continued unrest, with potential danger to American organisations and to the security of neighbouring parts of India.'

The roots of the communist movement in Nepal can be traced back to 1949, when the Communist Party of Nepal was founded under the leadership of the late Pushpa Lal Shrestha, who emerged as an academic counterweight to the Nepali Congress. The Maoist movement has emerged against the background of this history. On 12 February 1996 the Communist Party of Nepal (Maoist), or CPN-Maoist, started its so-called 'people's war' (jana yuddha) to bring about the collapse of what it called reactionary state power and to institute a new people's republic.

The CPN-Maoist is one of several splinter groups of the Communist Party of Nepal that believes in the ideals of the

Chinese Cultural Revolution as represented nowadays by the Revolutionary Internationalist Movement (RIM). The CPN-Maoist came into being when the political wing of Nepal's radical left parties, the Samyukta Jana Morcha Nepal (SJMN) or United People's Front Nepal, split in late 1993. At that time the SJMN had been the third-strongest force in the Pratinidhi Sabha (House of Representatives), with nine MPs. The splinter group around Pushpa Kamal Dahal, better known as Comrade Prachanda, now calls itself CPN-Maoist.

Their (Maoist) goals are to overthrow the bureaucrat-capitalist class and state system, which they see as dependent on and serving imperialism; uproot semi-feudalism; and drive out imperialism. To do this, the CPN (Maoist) is applying Mao's strategy of protracted people's war - establishing base areas in the countryside, aiming to surround the cities, seize nationwide power and establish a new democratic republic as a step toward building a new socialist society. Their struggle is seen as part of the world proletarian revolution.

These forces have ideologically integrated with their counterparts in the communist world and also with the strong Marxist-Leninist diaspora in Latin America and India. Maoist communist revolutionaries from Peru, the Philippines and India (Andhra Pradesh, West Bengal and Bihar) are linked with the Revolutionary Internationalist Movement (RIM), which is preparing the ground for the ultimate coming together of communist revolutionaries throughout the world. The Revolutionary Internationalist Movement is the developing centre of the world's 'purist' communist forces and is struggling for the formation of a Communist International of a new type based on Marxism-Leninism-Maoism. It is believed that they have more than fraternal links with the Maoist Communist Centre (MCC), which operates in the Indian states of Bihar, and the PWG in Andhra Pradesh.

Inside sources reveal that the Maoist leadership is hiding

in India. It is also no secret that India's Maoist groups acquire weapons for the Nepali rebels, provide them safe houses on Indian territory and have trained them in the use of explosives and landmines. Such acknowledgement - open or otherwise - has little or no significance unless it ultimately leads to the dismantling of the much-talked-about nexus between Nepalese Maoists and Indian extremist groups such as the Naxalites, ULFA or the People's War Group. Indirectly, the Nepali army is already fighting what can be called a cross-border war.

Washington does not have major interests in Nepal, but analysts believe it will be indirectly affected by increased volatility in India's northeast, bordering on China. It will also be concerned about the likely deterioration in the human-rights situation. The most immediate US concern, however, will be the security threat to its organisations and citizens. Michael E. Malinowski, US ambassador to Nepal, says that Maoism or the so-called 'people's war' is fundamentally the same as terrorism elsewhere - whether members of Shining Path, Abu Sayyaf, the Khmer Rouge or al-Qaeda. They are, according to him, radicals who seek to impose their narrow views and beliefs on others, despite the popular will of those they seek to influence or convert.

Nepal, in the past, has left no stone unturned to maintain an even-handed relationship between India and China. It has very close trade and industrial links with India, and there is considerable movement of people across their porous border. India has traditionally viewed Nepal's stability as an important component of its own security and has reacted sharply to any military connection between Nepal and China. Observers point out that the worst Indo-Nepal crisis in modern history arose out of India's harsh reaction to reports of a military sales agreement between Nepal and China.

India has traditionally had the upper hand due to manifold potential pressure points on Nepal. These, analysts believe, include the security provisions of the 1950 Treaty of Friendship, under which New Delhi can act in response to Kathmandu's request for military help, and Nepal's reliance on India for import and export transit. India's best strategy, says a strategic analyst, may be the one it has already begun: strengthening border defence and dealing with its own insurgencies. 'Because China's policy will probably be driven by India's, India should seek to avoid sharp reactions that could spark greater Chinese involvement,' he adds.

China has always had a special interest in Nepal, as it has served as a transit point for Tibetan refugees headed for India, most notably including the Karmapa Lama, who was granted asylum by India. Observers feel China's main concern is the potential use of Nepal as a safe haven by the Free Tibet movement. Kavre, Dolakha and Sindhupalchok districts, hotbeds of Maoist insurgency, lie along the 120-kilometre Araniko highway connecting Nepal and China, built in the 1960s with Chinese help despite India's protestations. Analysts also point out that there is at present no evidence of official Chinese support for the Nepalese Maoists, although an upsurge in Tibetan activities in Nepal could make the Maoists an attractive tool for retaliation.

A senior political scientist observes: 'That Maoist insurgency has survived six years and continues to enter new phases is in itself a clear indication that the movement is no longer a temporary phenomenon without social bases.' Insiders believe that the bureaucratic approach of viewing the Maoist movement as 'an activity of individual killing and pure terrorism' has not helped resolve the problem. When the movement began, it relied on extortion; as it expanded, it became more sophisticated. letters were sent to businessmen and contractors to donate money; later, they made it mandatory for teachers, civil servants, contractors and other professionals living in villages to pay a certain amount to the Maoist administration as revenue.

The insurgents have lately established themselves in urban areas. The Maoists have reportedly been engaged in mobilising workers to help local people with various construction and development projects. Reports from Nepal suggest they help villagers with crop planting and harvesting, and also with cleaning to win influence and support. The Maoist system of governance is based on equal access to resources and equal rights for all. They have, according to media reports, set up 'People's Courts' that look into cases, give verdicts and direct local commanders to take judicial action. The Maoist insurgents, many believe, have a lot of popular support in villages that are reeling under poverty and unemployment.

Another notable feature of the Maoist movement is the degree of women's participation in guerrilla ranks. Women's political involvement in the past had been limited to the electoral arena, particularly in voting and occasional candidacy. It has come as a big surprise to observers that Nepali women have joined the guerrilla organisation. According to one estimate, about 35 per cent of Maoist guerrillas are women, a new phenomenon that has emerged in Nepal.

Despite the extension of the state of emergency, Nepali state forces have not been able to inflict irreparable damage on the insurgents. Sometimes it is a delay in the arrival of reinforcements; sometimes it is a lack of coordination between the army and police. Most of the time, it is poor communications and faulty intelligence – areas where they have slipped up. The government apparently continues to treat the intelligence service and other pressing security issues with some disdain, which, according to many observers, is dangerous. A political analyst observes: 'The state of emergency is in itself no magic wand. It needs to be supplemented by good intelligence and good tactics. It is also a breathing spell that should be used to take a hard look at dialogue.'

Nepali strategic planners have failed to evolve a strategy by which people would stop providing sanctuaries to guerrillas.

This, observers point out, could have been done through a substantial economic development package directed to people in the initial stages of the uprising. Media reports also indicate that the relief package the government has allocated after so many killings has become largely irrelevant. Counter-insurgency actions require civil-military coordination in which clean civil administrators are expected to disburse economic development packages. A strategic analyst observes: 'Nepal's problem is not the Maoist war but an entrenched coalition of corrupt politicians and bureaucrats that profits from the Maoist war. The economic relief package announced to combat insurgency could likely be yet another opportunity for corrupt civilian as well as military authorities to embezzle funds.' He adds that counter-insurgency measures, if applied and executed by clean hands, will help minimise the distribution crisis, which in turn will help neutralise popular support for the guerrillas. Otherwise, many believe, it remains a protracted problem, and there is no way to prevent a Maoist revolution. The government forces, under the present policies, could win a couple of battles here and there, but they will never win the war.

7.2 IS THE US GOING THE USSR WAY?

January 2003

The United States has 37,000 troops and more than 90 installations scattered across the length and breadth of South Korea under a mutual defence treaty. Nevertheless, this presence has long been a source of antagonism for communities near the military bases.

On 13 June 2002, a US armoured vehicle hit and killed Shin Hyo-sun and Shim Mi-seon, both 14, who were walking on the shoulder of a road on their way to a friend's birthday party in the northern city of Uijeongbu. Since then, there has been a growing sense of anti-Americanism gaining momentum - not that the phenomenon is new, but what has angered Koreans is that the two US soldiers, Walker and Nino, were acquitted by a special American military court.

This incident has led to renewed calls for the removal of all US troops from the Korean peninsula. Of the 500 or so crimes committed by off-duty American soldiers, less than 1 per cent of the cases have made it to Korean courts. The rest have been handled by America's military courts, with many of the soldiers receiving only warnings or community service.

The nature and conduct of America's foreign policy over the past half-century, focusing particularly on the decade after the demise of the Soviet Union in 1991, needs to be put in perspective to understand the current trends emerging in the post-Cold War, unipolar world order. The scheme of things that will unfold in the twenty-first century will no doubt be driven by the fallout from the latter half of the twentieth century - consequences of the Cold War, with crucial American decisions forming the nucleus of this anger and reprisal.

In the present context, the combative approach adopted by the Bush regime, calling for regime change in Iraq, does not come as a big surprise. What has made the task difficult are the repercussions the US is likely to face down the line from radical Muslim groups for invading a Muslim country like Iraq.

On the other hand, if one takes a more pragmatic approach, the other member of what America describes as the 'axis of evil' or 'rogue states', North Korea, is not alleged merely to possess chemical and biological weapons (as in the case of Iraq) but has a full-fledged nuclear programme going on right under America's nose – of course with the clandestine support of an able ally of America in its global war on terrorism: Pakistan!

Incidentally, Saddam Hussein, the president of Iraq, was armed and backed to the hilt by the Reagan administration so long as he was at war with Khomeini's Iran; it is now ironic and amusing that all these men who were once listed as 'assets' of America's key covert services are at the receiving end once their utility in serving American interests has come to an end.

Since the Gulf War, the United States has steadily maintained around 35,000 troops in Saudi Arabia. Devoutly Muslim citizens of that kingdom see their presence as a humiliation to the country and an affront to their religion. Dissident Saudis have launched attacks against Americans and against the Saudi regime itself. It is in this context that one needs to examine renewed attacks on military facilities in the country in which scores of American soldiers have been killed.

Should the present American and Saudi Arabian establishments pursue their present policies, it is most likely that the Saudi monarchy will be overthrown and a fundamentalist, anti-American government will assume power in Riyadh. But American foreign policy remains unchanged; instead of withdrawing from a place where a US presence is only making a 'dangerous' situation 'worse', the United States continues to overlook the obvious.

The United States, even a decade after the demise of its Cold War foe, the USSR, continues to deploy awesome military might worldwide, so that for its adversaries only an 'asymmetric strategy', to borrow an expression from the Pentagon dictionary, has any chance of success.

Osama bin Laden, the leading suspect as mastermind behind the carnage of 11 September, was propped up by the CIA like so many other extreme fundamentalists among the mujahideen in Afghanistan from at least 1984, including building in 1986 the training complex and weapons storage tunnels around the Afghan city of Khost, where bin Laden trained many of the 35,000 Arabs.

Bin Laden's Khost complex was the one that, at President Bill Clinton's orders, was hit on 20 August 1998 with cruise missiles in retaliation for bin Laden's attacks of 7 August 1998 on the American embassies in Kenya and Tanzania. For once, the CIA knew where the targets were, since it had built them.

The retribution against the US is a fallout of ill-conceived, short-term, invariably illegitimate US covert actions aimed at overthrowing foreign administrations or assisting in the initiation of state terrorist operations against target populations. The people of America are unlikely to know what was done in their name, but those on the receiving end surely do - including the people of Iran (1953), Guatemala (1954), Cuba (1959-60), Congo (1960), Brazil (1964), Indonesia (1965), Vietnam (1961-73), Laos (1961-73), Cambodia (1961-73), Chile (1973), El Salvador and Nicaragua (1980s), Iraq (1991 to the present) and very probably Greece (1967), to name only the obvious cases.

American bombing operations of recent decades in Vietnam, Laos, Cambodia, Iraq, Serbia and Kosovo will almost certainly produce unintended negative consequences throughout the Islamic and developing worlds. Moderate Muslim governments, especially in Saudi Arabia, Turkey,

Egypt and Pakistan, will almost certainly face growing internal dissent and, if recent election trends in some of these states are any indication, America's task becomes all the more difficult with the emergence of a radical anti-American bandwagon.

In the opinion of a leading expert on American foreign policy, the US is embarked on a path not so dissimilar to that of the former Soviet Union a decade ago. He observes: 'It collapsed for three reasons - internal economic contradictions, imperial overstretch, and an inability to reform. In every sense, we were by far the wealthier of the two Cold War superpowers, so it will certainly take longer for similar afflictions to do their work. But it is nowhere written that the United States, in its guise as an empire dominating the world, must go on forever.'

The calamitous proceedings of the first year of the new millennium not only cast serious doubts on the United States' self-proclaimed role as 'indispensable nation' and 'only remaining superpower' but also raise serious reservations and new perils for other governments that were suddenly asked by President George W. Bush whether they were 'for' or 'against' the United States in its 'war on terror'.

7.3 A TALE OF TWO FUGITIVES

January 2003

Once upon a time, there lived two fugitives - poles apart, yet strikingly alike. Both held democratic establishments to ransom and committed the most inhumane acts, dispatching innocent victims by the worst possible means. Nothing could stop their despicable and diabolical deeds unless they were caught - to borrow an expression - dead or alive. Both claimed widespread support, which lent them the motivation to continue their war against humankind.

One is known to inhabit jungles somewhere in the Western Ghats, at the tri- junction of Tamil Nadu, Karnataka and Kerala in southern India. The other's last known address lies somewhere in Afghanistan or Pakistan - though half the time, there is confusion about which territory either fugitive currently occupies. To be safe, one might assume they live 'on the cusp', as astrologers say. Yes - and there are no prizes for guessing - we are talking about Osama bin Laden and our very own Koose Muniswamy Veerappan.

To bracket Veerappan alongside Osama may not sound quite right at first. After all, Osama has beaten him hands down in recognition and notoriety - currency a fugitive craves above all else. In both cases, video cassettes and audio tapes serve as vital props. The similarities do not end there. Both cultivate idiosyncratic appearances: Veerappan sports what may be the most unusual signature moustache in the world, which he twirls when angry, while Osama's flowing beard, streaked with grey, lends him the divine, spiritual aura he needs to captivate his followers.

One often wonders how these men would look stripped of their trappings. In Osama's case, we have some idea from early photographs, but with Veerappan we have nothing - save perhaps some clever digital imaging - to help us picture a clean-shaven version of the man.

Both fugitives come from sharply contrasting backgrounds. Osama, now 44, was born into an extremely wealthy family. The son of a Yemeni-born owner of a leading Saudi construction company, he is believed to have inherited as much as $300 million on his father's death. Until his worldview took a fanatical turn, he lived comfortably, enjoying life to the fullest. Veerappan, by contrast, now around 50, was born into a poor family in Gopinatham village in the Kollegal forest area of Karnataka. Early hardships, coupled with latent ruthlessness, turned him into India's most-wanted fugitive. Determined to do better than his cattle-grazing village friends, he killed his first elephant in his early teens. The rest is history.

Osama has the dubious distinction of being the first fugitive in pursuit of whom the mighty Uncle Sam has launched a satellite or two. As for Veerappan, the Government of India and the Government of Tamil Nadu have, for God knows how long, dispatched elite task forces to track him down in the forests. For 35 years, in self-imposed exile, Veerappan has been on the move, his legs unfatigued despite years of trekking through dense jungle - and that too, believe it or not, in bathroom slippers. Unlike Osama, who was stripped of his citizenship, Veerappan still enjoys full Indian citizenship. Saudi Arabia revoked bin Laden's nationality in 1994, citing his opposition to the Saudi King, and expelled him. He fled to Khartoum, Sudan, where he owns several businesses, but under US pressure was expelled again in 1996. He then moved to Afghanistan and is now on the run.

Veerappan faces over 150 cases and is accused of 119 murders. He smuggles ivory and sandalwood worth millions of rupees - partly, one suspects, to keep himself occupied. Lately, he has resorted to kidnapping and extortion, perhaps seeking companionship. In his most recent episode, the outcome could not have been grimmer: former Karnataka Minister H. Nagappa, 66, held captive for 106 days, became the latest victim of the elusive forest brigand. This is neither his first nor, in all likelihood, his last act of brutality. In the past he has also held hostage an ageing matinee idol.

Osama, by contrast, does not carry out attacks himself; he commands far greater resources. Yet the bottom line is the same. He has been linked to the 1992 hotel bombing in Yemen that killed two Australians; the 1995 car bomb in Riyadh, Saudi Arabia; the 1995 truck bomb in Dhahran that killed 19 US servicemen; and the 1995 assassination attempt on Egyptian President Hosni Mubarak. Bin Laden has been directly connected to the 7 August 1998 bombings of US embassies in Nairobi, Kenya, and Dar es Salaam, Tanzania, which killed 224 people; the October 2000 attack on the USS Cole in Yemen; and, most infamously, the atrocities that brought down the World Trade Centre. Members of his network also penetrated the high-security fortress of the Pentagon.

Both fugitives nurture ideologies they fervently protect and propagate. Bin Laden has long exploited anti-American, anti-Western and anti-Israel sentiments as justification for his attacks. He has been outspoken on these themes, using the pan-Arabic satellite channel Al Jazeera to issue theological rulings calling on Muslims to attack Americans and threatening terror against related targets. Citing the defeat of Soviet forces in Afghanistan, he has consistently declared the United States vulnerable to jihad waged by Islamic forces.

Not to be outdone, Veerappan fancies himself the sole protector of Tamilians. After the Rajkumar kidnapping, he proclaimed himself guardian of the rights of 60 million Tamils. He goes further, declaring - without batting an eyelid - that he could win an election hand down. He even dreams of a career in public life, a fantasy rooted in his belief that he enjoys widespread sympathy among Tamils.

When the perennial Cauvery river water dispute between Karnataka and Tamil Nadu turned violent, Veerappan raided a police station inside Karnataka to proclaim his solidarity with the Tamil cause and express his contempt for Chief Minister S. M. Krishna and his administration.

Believe it or not, both fugitives command sizeable followings that, if not growing, show no sign of dwindling. Osama draws support from right-wing ultra-fundamentalist Muslims who sincerely believe it is their moral duty to attack non-believers, whom they consider the greatest threat to Islam. Veerappan's story is not so different. He is known to have helped the poor in times of hardship, financed marriages and donated to temple construction. Unsurprisingly, he is worshipped and seen as a benefactor. Unlike Osama, Veerappan has had no formal schooling, yet that has not prevented him from mastering wily, fox-like cunning - qualities he displays more often than anyone would wish.

Both men are known to leave a lasting impression on those who encounter them. Osama's discourses have, time and again, effectively lured recruits to his cause. If the forest grapevine is to be believed, those who have spent time with Veerappan have suffered from Stockholm syndrome, in which captives come to empathise with their captor. He is also known for his booming voice and an endless supply of jokes to entertain his hostages. Small wonder he remains at large.

Given their warped logic, to expect either fugitive to return voluntarily to civilised society any time soon would be naive. If we are serious about apprehending them before they wreak further havoc, we must intercept them at sea and relieve them of their deadly cargo. Sink the ship, if necessary, but for heaven's sake, do not wait for it to dock. If we truly wish to break this deadlock, the most effective cure is drastic surgery.

7.4 THE LOST VALLEY

July 2002

The fate of beauty is to be fought over,

She is the constant nymph,

At every wedding, beauty's the bride;

Each victor's fate is surrender

At Kashmir's toe-shaped pride.

Not enough blood in the world

To taint thy immaculate snow;

A ray of the rising sun

Can touch off a bashful glow.

– Krishnalal Shridharan

Kashmir was all smiles. Snow-capped peaks glistened in the sun. Lakes, myriad murmuring springs, emerald-green turf, the lattice-work of tall, slender poplars and haunting groves of chinars, towering snow-clad mountains led by Nanga Parbat - all combined to make it the playground of the gods. It cannot be called a rock-bound prison; the mountains stand guard not to keep Kashmiris in but to keep unwelcome outsiders out. It is a bastion that opens its gates to friends. For trekkers, Kashmir has long been the ultimate paradise - a place to disappear into the mountains, to enjoy tranquility and serenity, to commune with nature in ways found nowhere else. The topography, from the Shivalik hills of Jammu to the jagged peaks of Ladakh, is a geographer's delight. Nowhere in the world can one witness such dramatic geographic transformation in so short a distance: diverse flora and fauna, Alpine pastures nestled among snow-clad peaks, air so pure and oxygenated it seems to cleanse the soul.

It was my final year at high school, in the summer of 1989, when the first signs of separatist and secessionist movements became evident in Kashmir. Sporadic bombings and killings were becoming the order of the day. Our school had a long tradition of sending its graduating batch on a summer trek, an event keenly awaited by all. Little did we know, as teenagers embarking on a rugged Himalayan adventure amid high mountains, lofty peaks and endless glaciers, that these very landscapes would, within a decade, become hubs of terrorist activity - the so-called 'liberated zones'.

On a fine sunny morning, we set out by bus from our school in Srinagar to Ducksum in south Kashmir, a journey of roughly four hours. Ducksum, famed for its scenic beauty, lies 40 kilometres from the district headquarters at Anantnag. Along with Kokernag and Achabal, it had long been a favourite destination for school children in the Valley undertaking their annual excursions.

The place was to serve as our base camp for a 14-day expedition. In the end, thanks to fine weather, we completed the trek in less than 11 days. Our first major challenge was scaling the Margan Pass, situated 4,430 meters above sea level, from Mati Guran. The journey was memorable yet frightening - thick fog enveloped us as we made steady progress despite a few mishaps. At one point a mule tumbled down a steep slope, and rumours spread that it carried all our precious tinned food. We were devastated! The local porters assisting us helped rescue the mule and retrieve the entire load.

We had heard many stories about the sensational, breathtaking views of the Wadwan valley, but nothing compared to what sprawled beneath us as we crested the pass. We were all mesmerised. Despite having lived in Kashmir, we had never encountered such innocent beauty. Everything looked untouched, serene and calm - a feeling that creeps up on you once in a lifetime.

Kishtwar, in the Doda district of the Jammu region, comprises four major areas. The Wadwan region is one of the remotest, its villages tucked away 3,000 metres above sea level in dense forests, with no roads, telephones or electricity. It remains one of the poorest parts of the state and lies a five-day trek from the tehsil headquarters at Kishtwar – the same time it took us to reach it from south Kashmir. The valley spreads from the villages of Hanzi and Inshan and comprises 14 settlements in all: Inshan, Virwan, Afti and Mingli were among those we passed through during our trek. The valley boasts scenic spots such as Tuiller, Nopachi, Marwah, Tata Pani and Dashbal, many rich in trout with a unique rainbow hue. The Marwah River flows through the centre of the valley, flanked by lush meadows.

More than a decade later, the valley systems of Wadwan and Marwah that we explored as schoolchildren have become safe havens for militants in Jammu & Kashmir. Dacchan and Paddar valleys to the south are likewise insecure. The terrorist groups that executed a series of communal massacres in Doda from 1996 onwards, as well as those that carried out attacks on Amarnath pilgrims since the summer of 2000, are all believed to have retreated into the safety of Wadwan.

We spent one night in the Inshan valley and another at Virwan village, where we had the opportunity to interact with local villagers. We learnt that there was only one matriculate in the entire valley – a man who had set up a primary school with government aid. The price of essential commodities in this remote, inaccessible area was five times higher than elsewhere.

A reporter who visited the area 12 years after our expedition wrote: 'On 13 April 2001, an SOG-Rashtriya Rifles team launched its first Wadwan operation and claimed five terrorists at the village of Virwan. On the night of 20 May, seven more terrorists were killed at Rikkenwas, followed by one more at Pasar Nullah on 11 June. During post-monsoon operations, two terrorists were killed at Inshan in October, and in November another three were killed at Mingli.' Media reports also indicate that terrorism brought to a halt work on the road being built from Kokernag to Wadwan in 1988.

Our next major challenge, worthy of special mention, was scaling the Giulol Pass at 4,410 metres above sea level. We started very early in the morning, but by noon had made little progress; the climb was steep and our rucksacks added to our discomfort. Little did we know what awaited us at the top. The weather was freezing cold, and we were astounded to find a 12-kilometre-long glacier – a distance we had to cross to begin our descent towards Sheshnag, one of the base camps for the Amarnath yatra. Our blistered feet compounded our woes, and it took the better part of three hours to cross the freezing expanse of snow.

One columnist later wrote: 'This April, for example, the Army stopped Wadwan horsemen from crossing the Pir Panjal to cater to pilgrims travelling to the Amarnath shrine. The decision was taken after terrorist attacks on pilgrims fuelled fears that the high passes might be used for further strikes.'

By the time we reached Sheshnag late in the evening, a cold, icy storm had picked up. We had no option but to abandon the idea of erecting our own tents and sought shelter in an abandoned stable to protect ourselves from freezing to death. Brandy and hot tomato soup were in abundant supply throughout the night.

We made one more overnight halt at the now-famous Betab Valley – so named because the film Betab was shot there – near Chandanwari. We reached the end of our expedition three days ahead of schedule, giving us enough time to tend to blistered feet and aching limbs. At the trek's conclusion, we left Pahalgam for Srinagar, leaving behind the valley tucked in the magnificent Pir Panjal range – forever, never to return again!

www.ingramcontent.com/pod-product-compliance
Lightning Source LLC
Chambersburg PA
CBHW050015170726
48282CB00025B/412
* 9 7 8 9 3 5 6 5 5 4 5 0 4 *